D1505911

McCLANE'S
GREAT FISHING AND HUNTING LODGES
OF NORTH AMERICA

Golden Horn Lodge, Bristol Bay, Alaska.

McCLANE'S GREAT FISHING AND HUNTING LODGES OF NORTH AMERICA

Photographed by George W. Gardner
Edited with an Introduction by A. J. McClane
Text by Terry Berger and Roberta Gardner
Designed and Produced by Robert R. Reid

HOLT, RINEHART AND WINSTON, *New York*

Special thanks to J. D. Adams
for editorial research and for providing
special phrases and descriptions
embodied in the text.

Map by Anthony St. Aubyn

Copyright © 1984 by Holt, Rinehart and Winston
All rights reserved, including the right to reproduce
this book or portions thereof in any form.
Published by Holt, Rinehart and Winston,
383 Madison Avenue, New York, New York 10017.
Published simultaneously in Canada by Holt, Rinehart
and Winston of Canada, Limited.

Library of Congress Cataloging in Publication Data
McClane, A. J. (Albert Jules), 1922–
    McClane's Great fishing and hunting lodges of North
America.

    1. Hunting lodges—United States.   2. Hunting lodges—
Canada.   3. Fishing lodges—United States.   4. Fishing
lodges—Canada.   I. Berger, Terry.   II. Gardner, Roberta.
III. Title.   IV. Title: Great fishing and hunting
lodges of North America.
SK41.M38 1984   799'.025'7   83-22814

ISBN: 0-03-061339-6

First Edition

A Robert R. Reid production

Printed in the United States of America

10 9 8 7 6 5 4 3 2 1

ISBN 0-03-061339-

Contents

Introduction

I N THIS MODERN AGE we risk becoming drones by choice or chance, breathing the stale smell of routine in a nine-to-five world, seen through a permanently sealed office window. Even troglodyte man could walk out of his cave and find a constantly changing landscape, if not a dinosaur chop. Hunting and fishing are great anodynes for dulled senses, if only because you will go places and examine things that would otherwise escape your notice. My spring tonic for the past quarter century has been a journey to south-eastern Maine to enjoy smallmouth bass fishing in the myriad pine-clad glacial lakes, in the company of beaver, moose, osprey, and eagle. The catch can be phenomenal at times, but I keep just one bass for that noontime marriage with a potato and onion in melted butter—a simple woodfire ceremony that always restores my sense of continuity. Yet the truth is, I also suffer from a summer, fall, and winter syndrome—like a periodic itch between the shoulder blades that can't be reached. The cure may be tarpon in the Florida Keys, a Mexican duck hunt, the awesome sight of an elk meadow in the first snow, when the herd has come down from the hills, or the sound of leaping salmon in a pristine Alaskan or Labrador river.

In 1952, my wife Patti and I spent our honeymoon tenting in Alaska. It was a great adventure, and the fact that we are still married after expeditions to the wilds of the Congo, the Amazon, the Orinoco, Tierra del Fuego, and similar far flung destinations in the outdoors is testimony to her endurance. Fortunately, in recent years there has been a proliferation of resorts catering to peripatetic sportsmen and, with jet travel, my itch can be scratched more easily than ever before.

The first hunting and fishing club in the New World was the Schuylkill Fishing Company, founded at Schuylkill, Pennsylvania, in 1732, a very private and social enterprise to this day, and no longer in a location suitable to the pursuit of fish and game. However, it was the prototype for similar gathering places that evolved during the nineteenth century in farm houses, ranches, log cabins, boarding houses, and tent camps across the land. Those of us who hunt and fish are a dedicated lot, and nobody knows this better than the kindred souls who proudly toil at what can only be described as the work of making an intricately run home away from home for sportsmen and sportswomen.

Operating a sporting camp must be a rewarding career, not from the standpoint of money, because few lodge owners ever claim great wealth as a future objective, or make it in the here and now. Indeed, the complexity of things that can go wrong, particularly in a remote location with a long supply line, makes running a sporting camp a risky undertaking at best. Over the years, I have seen many camps go bankrupt, and those that have survived are often in an area where the rate of occupancy can fluctuate wildly. However, great lodges are never bereft of guests. Statistically, there are thousands of hunting and fishing camps in North America, but many of these offer little more than a lumpy mattress, an outhouse, and a bit of moose hair in the stew. Only a small percentage could be called great, not merely because of the amenities and the quality of the sport but the professionalism of the management. In this book you will meet Bud and Holly Hodson at Golden Horn Lodge, Maggie Gary and Ron McMillan at Bristol Bay Lodge, Jerry Bricker at Frontier Lodge,

Peter McVey at Corbett Lake Country Inn, Stan Leen at Leen's Lodge, and many other celebrated hosts who orchestrate their business with an attention to detail that is rare in these lax times.

It is unfortunate that only twenty lodges can be described in this book, yet, we offer a fair sampler of what North America has to offer. We have not awarded stars or compared one lodge to another and have provided a cross-section of places, expensive and inexpensive, remote or just off the highway, for the family, or to visit alone. I think the best indication of the seductiveness of lodge living was the journey of urban photographer George Gardner. After we decided what we wanted to cover, George disappeared for two years—and never even sent me a postcard!

A. J. McClane

Editor-at-Large
Sports Afield

9

GOLDEN

HORN LODGE

Bristol Bay,
Alaska

Spectacular fishing amid spectacular scenery.

BRISTOL BAY has been called the "world's greatest salmon factory," and Golden Horn Lodge is located in its wilderness littoral where tundra, interlaced with rivers and streams, stretches to the horizon. Here, moose and caribou live undisturbed, and brown bear and arctic loons perform at the lodge's doorstep.

Mile after mile of untracked forests host unnamed places on this two-million-acre preserve in the Wood River-Tikchik Lakes region of Bristol Bay, Alaska. It is an area visited by few, and free from the traces of man. The scenery and sports fishing are spectacular.

At the Golden Horn all the luxuries await you: fine food, comfortable interiors lavishly hung with mounted heads and pelts, a warm and welcoming hearth, and a bar. Built with logs and beams, the lodge is carpeted throughout its two stories. Maps and trophies cover the walls, and in addition to a game table there is a small collection of books, as well as a work table for fly-tiers to invent new patterns or restock old ones. Considering the size of the fish, the attrition on flies can be phenomenal.

Bud and Holly Hodson, natives of southern California and residents of Anchorage off-season, mastermind the services that the Golden Horn offers between June and October each year. Holly has a thoroughly capable kitchen staff, and daily maid service is prompt and efficient. Bud is responsible for organizing the fishing parties, and he pilots his own plane as well. The Golden Horn's three aircraft, many small boats, and talented crew of guides are all under his supervision.

12

Guests arrive with great expectations; they leave with lifetime memories.

Guide Ludin Coward oversees J. D. Adams hooking a pink salmon on the Nuyakuk River, forty minutes flight from the lodge.

Shimmering firelight shows off a prize Dolly Varden trophy in the dining room.

Each evening, and again in the morning, Bud Hodson and the staff determine weather conditions and set the day in motion. They assign fishing locations and issue equipment, depending upon individual interest. If the sky is clear, three de Havilland Beavers are ready to go, with skilled bush pilots, to cover a wilderness area greater than the state of West Virginia. Carrying a small number of anglers, each plane takes off in a different direction, and maneuvers deftly when landing at the fishing sites. All sites offer different fishing experiences in secluded areas. The Igulapak and Togiak Rivers offer superb fly-fishing for rainbow trout, grayling, and Arctic char.

Actually, the number of species available almost seems like an excess. There are also Dolly Varden, lake trout, northern pike, coho salmon, chinook salmon, sockeye salmon and pink salmon at various locations. In fact, this watershed receives the most extensive salmon runs in the world. Millions of fish return year after year to spawn, and it is an awesome sight to see streams running red with spawning salmon late in the season.

Talented marine biologists, as well as outstanding sportsmen have tested their skills in these fine streams: Chris Child and his special Bitch Creek fly; Ludin Coward, who broke the world record marlin catch off the Florida coast when he was sixteen; and Bud Hodson himself, a gifted fisherman in his own right.

Outcamps are situated at some point along the rivers, where tents are set up and fires lit. Here, for weeks on end, guides live like trappers of old, except for Coleman stoves and Duracell batteries. The guides are not only helpful in perfecting fishing techniques, but they also focus unfamiliar eyes on the wonders of the North country. Pistols and rifles are carried for protection from bears, so safety is maintained in the midst of adventure.

The flight back is often sensational, with moose and caribou

Expert Chris Child ties his favorite fly at the lodge's fly table.

Bud Hodson, part-owner and manager.

crossing the tundra in plain view. Back inside the lodge, liquor, beer, and wine are served. The comfortable living room seduces the weary sportsman, stoves are blazing in the kitchen, and guests reuniting bring exciting fishing tales to the forthcoming lodge-style dinner.

The dinner bell rings. The food is served. The succulent prime rib, the tender, char-broiled steak, and the festive roast chicken will long be remembered, along with the home-baked bread, pastries, and biscuits that the chef prepares daily.

A golden view at noon of the Golden Horn Lodge on Lake Mitchalk.

BRISTOL

BAY LODGE

Bristol Bay,
Alaska

19

Where sportsmanship and conservation go hand-in-hand.

THREE HUNDRED AND FIFTY AIR MILES southwest of Anchorage lies the huge Bristol Bay watershed. One part of this vast region contains fourteen major lakes and numerous crystal-clear rivers and inlets. The unsurpassed scenery, the incredible fishing, and the grandeur of the locale add up to make it the ultimate wilderness experience. Because of its inaccessibility by anything other than float-equipped aircraft, this rugged, beautiful area is visited by fewer than one thousand sportsmen every year.

The massive runs of chinook, sockeye, chum, pink, and coho salmon, as well as sea-run Dolly Varden, make the Bristol Bay fishing adventure an education in migratory fish. Twelve species of fish either inhabit these waters or return here to spawn and die, making the area a true angler's haven at any time during the season.

Maggie Gary toasting guests on the dock with her traditional brandy. At right is Bud Winter, Olympic coach and ardent fisherman.

20

The lodge's main lounge.

Resident fresh-water fish include rainbow trout, lake trout, Arctic grayling, Arctic char, Dolly Varden, and northern pike. Fishing begins at Bristol Bay after ice-out in mid-May, and excellent fishing is possible until the winter cold fronts descend in October.

Proud of its firm stand regarding sportsmanship and conservation, Bristol Bay Lodge subscribes to the now widespread practice of catch-and-release angling. The area is protected under federal law, and managed through regulations enforced by the Alaska Department of Fish and Game. The owner of the Lodge, Maggie Garry, and the manager, Ron McMillan, feel strongly about their bountiful fishing grounds; they are fulfilling a trust to future generations by protecting a resource whose future is dependent upon man's wise and prudent judgment.

Maggie Garry has lived in Alaska for twenty-odd years. When she spins her yarns about the winters in Kotzebue with her children, and the constant lack of supplies, one quickly detects the spirit of this frontier. Over the years she has collected many books, magazines, and photographic journals, and her library in itself offers a small vacation. Maggie, who built Bristol Bay Lodge with her former husband, has run things since it began, and she is the

only hostess it has ever known. Her name is celebrated in toasts at other fishing lodges, and her way is simple and loving. Maggie Garry lives the life described in *Coming Into the Country,* John McPhee's book about Alaska.

Ron McMillan, the holder of several patents on gadgets and inventions, runs the shop at Bristol Bay Lodge. He flies, fishes, hunts, is an expert woodsman, and knows the in-and-outs of wilderness living. When guests arrive at Dillingham, Ron or one of his crew members will meet them at the airport. In twenty minutes they are landing on Lake Aleknagik in the Bay in front of the lodge, by the mysterious Kilbuck Mountains.

The lodge, with its full kitchen, picture-window living room, and surrounding cabins is a scenic wonder. Maggie and her dogs

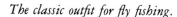

The classic outfit for fly fishing.

Maggie at the fly table constructing one of the many fly patterns available at the lodge. Her specialty, and a favorite of many, is called "Maggie's Horror."

greet deplaning guests with brandy served in traditional snifters on a silver tray. The boarding arrangements are quickly made, and after settling in, guests are lured to the lodge itself.

Dinner is always being made, and an enticing smorgasbord is featured. Austin, the head chef, makes sure of satisfying the slightest yen for more of this or less of that. By the time the week is over, guests are so pleased they want to abduct him, and no wonder! Not only is he skillful in the kitchen, but his Colorado-born disposition exudes a Rocky Mountain high.

Each night of the week features a different spread, with the usual appetizers. The burning wood in the fireplace melds with the smells of the kitchen and envelops the grounds around the lodge. A walk prior to dinnertime can be most relaxing and stimulating to the appetite at this Alaskan retreat, where the air is superfine and super clear.

On Saturday night, a special steak dinner is served, with each guest selecting his own cut of meat. The large grill is set crackling and each person cooks his steak the way he likes it. There is a choice of wine. The barbecue symbolizes another completed week's stay at Bristol Bay, and the staff marks it with song.

Folks leave and new folks arrive. "We hope to remain a home for the world's fishermen, a place where they can return to year after year," Maggie says. They do.

24

Ron McMillan, at left in the photo, shown releasing a Dolly Varden.

The lodge flies parties of fishermen to outlying rivers, streams, and lakes—wherever the best fishing is. Above, at "Bear Hotel," so named because the bears gather there for fish too, a fishing party is seen returning to the plane for the trip back to the lodge, where a warm fire, hot drinks, and a fine dinner await them.

PLUM

MER'S LODGES

Great Bear Lake,
Northwest
Territories

Roughing it north of the Arctic Circle.

WITH COMPLETE OUTFITTING and arrangements taken care of by Plummer's Lodges, an expedition to this remote part of the world more than lives up to the wonderous expectations of anyone who may have ventured so far. Forty-seven miles north of the Arctic Circle, the red-roofed, white wooden buildings of "Chummy" Plummer's

"Lakers," the famous trout found in Great Bear Lake.

The wood-frame cabins of Great Bear Lake Lodge, the only settlement for hundreds of miles, and a welcome sight when one is returning from a day's fishing expedition.

fishing lodge sit on a tiny peninsula built out into the Great Bear Lake, the third largest in the world. Bordering on the tundra, the lake contains more than 10,000 square miles of water and is one hundred miles from the Arctic Ocean. It derives its name from the constellation Ursa Major, which, like the other constellations, can be seen in the clear Arctic skies better than anywhere else in the world.

During the wintertime, six-foot-thick ice forms on the lake. This cuts down on the life-generating sunlight and results in Arctic fish growing more slowly than their southern counterparts. Arctic grayling, the "sailfish" of the region, average two pounds, and are more of a challenge than the larger lake trout, which can grow to one hundred pounds, but presents little challenge.

Plummer's is built on the rounded tip of a peninsula, with the Narakay Mountains to the west. As the highest landmark on the lake, the mountains are used as guideposts, and, when not visible from the main camp, plans for the day's fishing are changed. Even experienced guides have been waylaid for the night, confused by fog in the widespread wilderness. This rarely happens and it would be nothing more than a memorable inconvenience, like sleeping on the bottom of the boat, until you can be found by the airplanes

Left: *Friday evening cocktail hour north of the Arctic Circle.* Below: *Looking towards the North Pole from the main lodge.*

31

in the morning. Once back at the lodge, brandy and a jacuzzi are waiting. Nothing serious really, but, after all, at sixty degrees latitude and one hundred and twenty degrees longitude, this is the adventure of a lifetime.

Planes are an integral part of the operation at Plummer's. From July through August, flights leaving from Winnipeg on Saturday mornings fly guests to the lodge's private airstrip in a Boeing 737. In addition to the chartered jet, they have their own de Havilland single-engine Otter and a Cessna 206—both float planes—used mostly in running errands to neighboring camps and flying fishing parties out to the grayling rivers.

Plummer's uses its own DC 3 for transporting sportsmen to the Tree River Camp at Coronation Bay on the Arctic Ocean. The flight takes an hour-and-a-half, and ends at the open tundra, the finest spot in the world for giant Arctic char fishing, facilitated by a host of Inuit guide services.

There are no trees at Plummer's outcamp on the Tree River: only the bluffs, the tundra, and the river's white rapids. There are well-made tents and a permanent building housing kitchen facilities for meals. The only other habitation nearby in this remote area is

Above: *Early morning preparations for the day's Great Bear fishing expedition.*
Right: *The guide prepares the mid-day shore lunch with freshly caught fish.*

OVERLEAF: *The Tree River Camp on Coronation Bay, seven miles from the Arctic Ocean. This fishing area is exclusive to Plummer, and holds the Arctic char record for the world.*

Left, above: *Canadian watercolor painter Colin Pain following his guide along the turbulent Tree River.*

Below: *Mark Stricker with his twenty-one pound Arctic char. In two days of fishing on Tree River he hooked eighteen and caught twelve char—a record for a seventeen-year-old.*

Arctic char, the largest caught during 1982.

a Canadian Fish and Game Department generator and storage shed used for Arctic testing.

Other than the occasional Mountie, who checks in every year, no one but Plummer's staff, the Inuit guides, and some lucky sportsmen have ever seen or conceived of such a glorious site. The turbulent Tree is even beyond the realm of a fishing trip fantasy. It is the ideal!

In 1981, the world record Arctic char was caught and tagged on the Tree River. At thirty-two pounds, it was a glorious, colorful trophy.

The land of the midnight sun is an astonishing sight. Like a single band of brilliant phosphorescence at the horizon, magnetizing upwards into diffusing, cooler light, the magic aura of the Northland reigns at Tree River.

FRONTIER

FISHING LODGE

Great Slave Lake,
Northwest
Territories

The finest thrills the North can offer a fly fisherman.

JERRY BRICKER'S Frontier Fishing Lodge sits on the eastern arm of Great Slave Lake, 115 miles from Yellowknife, near Snowdrift in Canada's Northwest Territories. Here, a maze of islands, reefs, and coves makes up an area of more than 11,000 square miles, Christie Bay and the Stark River being just two of the five magnificent fishing and scenic wonders at this twenty-year-old lodge.

No more than a mile long and only a few hundred feet across, the Stark River is a shallow and somewhat difficult stream to navigate, even for the Chipewyan guides. The Arctic grayling put on a spectacular display, clearing the water in bounding leaps. This northern acrobat, described as the flower of fishes, is unquestionably one of the world's most beautiful freshwater fish, and provides some of the finest thrills the North can offer a fly

Fishermen come and go as they please at Frontier Lodge. This view from the lodge's dock shows Great Slave Lake during rush hour.

40

fisherman. For the epicure, the grayling makes one of creation's most delicately flavored dishes.

Generally dark blue on the back and purple-gray on the sides, the Arctic Grayling's outstanding characteristic is its large, sail-

Building so far north is a major task, as everything has to be imported over vast distances, including the logs for the cabins.

Owner Jerry Bricker holding a rod canister from the supply plane.

like, highly-colored dorsal fin, which is blackish-gray with a bright red band on the upper edge and a scattering of blue and violet spots. Averaging between one and two pounds, fish have been caught weighing up to five. They will take wet or dry flies and some metal lures, but they have tender mouths and must be handled carefully on the line. For best sport, Charlie Cook, a world-class fisherman from Dallas, Texas, and a regular at the lodge, advises waiting until evening and fly casting along rocky or gravelly shorelines.

Christie Bay, a long, deep finger in Great Slave (which in places reaches 2,000 feet in depth), features lake trout ranging between ten and sixty pounds, caught mostly by trolling using spinning outfits with spoons such as the Dardevle and spinners, such as the

42

Left, above: *Charlie Cook, one of America's great sportsmen, happily relaxes in the lodge's club room.* Left: *Joe, a Snowdrift Indian and a guide at the lodge, shown netting a grayling.*

Cecil Hazzard, left, comes to Frontier Lodge to draw and sketch subjects for his paintings, and usually stays the whole summer. Here he is shown fishing with his good friend, Charlie Cook, who comes to catch Arctic grayling on the Stark River.

*Messrs. Cook and Hazzard
stop for a shore lunch.*

44   Mepps. The trout hit savagely and show a preference for red-on-white, silver, copper, gold, and yellow. Veteran anglers compare their behavior and fishing qualities to brook trout, who tend to fight near the surface, alternately diving and splashing in an effort to throw the lure.

The Snowdrift River and Murky Lake, Stark Lake, and Wild-bread Bay are the other locations that provide a variety of fishing at Frontier Lodge. Fishermen are limited to ten grayling, twenty whitefish, ten northern pike, and two lake trout, one of which may be a trophy, a fish of twenty-eight inches or more. Both Great Slave and Stark Lakes are designated trophy lakes.

Jerry Bricker, dapper and charismatic, is a native of Edmonton, Alberta, and is an excellent fisherman himself. His choice of flies includes various nymphs and wet flies such as the Black Gnat, Silver Doctor, Gray and Brown Hackle, and Light and Dark Cahill on a No. 10 or 12 hook. "If it weren't for all the fishin' . . ." he chides, ". . . this place would be damn relaxin'."

In addition to great food, the lodge features a Finnish sauna, warm, cheery fires, and a direct-dial telephone via satellite. The lodge generates its own power and is also equipped with a two-way radio. The dining room and kitchen are located in a separate

Fly casting for Arctic grayling on the Stark River. Charlie Cook maintains that the river is "the best place in the world to catch grayling."

building, and there is a new conference and recreation building, with seven bedrooms, for executive and family use. Additional log cabins are available for those who request more private quarters, and twenty-four guests can be catered to at any one time.

His Royal Highness Prince Charles stayed with the Brickers, and was reported to be very talented with the fly rod. Having learned his fishing skills on the legendary streams of England and Scotland, he acquitted himself well with a good catch, and was overwhelmed by the finest stretch of grayling water in the world. He was also taken with Mrs. Bricker's homemade croissants served to him each morning. In fact, he commanded his plane to return to the lodge upon discovering that a box of croissants for the Queen Mother had been left behind.

The lodge is noted for its cooking, and visitors from all over the world maintain it is as good as that offered in fine restaurants, with fresh fruit and vegetables flown in. Products from the lodge's own smokehouse add spice to the menu, which varies daily.

This is a spectacular wilderness retreat, pollution free and isolated, even from the mining industry. Its fishing is phenomenal and within easy reach of the lodge by boat. The only thing one wishes for here is more time.

CORBETT LAKE

COUNTRY INN

Merritt,
British Columbia

A classic setting for a Renaissance man.

WHETHER ONE IS an active fisherman, skier, gourmet, or overland tourist, Corbett Lake Country Inn is the ideal resort. Located in the heart of the Nicola Valley in south-central British Columbia, it lies about half-a-day's drive from Vancouver, just south of Kamloops.

Adjacent to Highway 5, the inn is a favorite among those who crave scenic drives. The road ascends into the foothills of the Cascade range, with its sub-Alpine grasslands, stands of fir, and ponderosa pine scattered over the open, rolling hills that are dotted with meadows of wildflowers. Elevations reach 3,500 feet in this semi-desert region of western Canada, where summer days are generally warm and evenings cool.

The three hundred and five acres, originally part of the Duke of Portland's ranch, have access to Corbett and Courtenay Lakes and is a featured spot for fishermen interested in Kamloops rainbow trout. No motorboats are allowed on the lakes, and those who stay at the resort utilize rowboats. The lakes' biosphere is being improved through the application of marine biology by Peter McVey, the inn's owner, who is assuring Corbett's future as a haven for rainbow trout.

From a wide range of experience, Peter has expert advice to

48

Right: Peter McVey, still dressed in his chef's clothes, giving a fly casting lesson on the lawn after dinner. Left: during the day, he is shown on the grounds with Blackie the dog and the classic '61 Jaguar.

Fishing expert Don McDiarmid demonstrates the ultimate in waders, especially suited to fishing in Corbett Lake.

offer, including the techniques of rod building. In the shop attached to his woodshed and garage, Peter's cluttered production bin holds an accumulation of tools and diagrams—everything he needs—plus a few inventions. His procedures may seem unusual, but the end result is a masterpiece. Peter calls it "caveman stuff," this crafting by hand, in the time consuming steps necessary to the construction of a fine bamboo rod. But masters like Bob Southwell, from whom Peter learned his craft back in England, continue to preserve the tradition in an era when space-age materials—boron and graphite—dominate the market.

The lodge hosts seminars regularly by two of Canada's most active fly fishermen, Tom Murray and Don McDiarmid. During

The newest, premier cabin on the grounds, with the best view of the lake.

51

the course of a weekend stay, a wealth of information is passed around about fishing, the kinds of hatches to anticipate, the techniques of fly casting, the selection of tackle, and the proper rod action, constructing the tapered leader, and selecting the correct size tippet. Here success is knowing the difference between a *Gammarus* and a *Hyalella* (both amphipod crustaceans). The fishing enthusiast learns to utilize all the resources available to him. Enthusiasts as well as experts, Tom and Don are great conservationists who advocate catch-and-release programs as one way of preserving the fishery.

Peter McVey is not only manager, but also the head chef at Corbett Lake. His chateaubriand and escalope de veale Elenkia are

Peter McVey in his workshop;
his bamboo rods are products
of the highest quality, much
coveted by fishermen.

outstanding, and, along with other gourmet dishes, are legendary in these parts.

After receiving a scholarship in 1955 to attend a major hotel cooking school in London, Peter apprenticed to the catering establishment of the Lord Mayor of London. With such a four-star background, it is no wonder he is a marvel who manages to make each meal a unique experience. In addition, his choice of wines is extensive, ranging from California Zinfandels and Italian Valpolicellos to French Burgundies and German whites.

Accommodations are composed of comfortable cedar cottages with all facilities. Several have fireplaces, and all have kitchens and wonderful views of the lake and hills beyond.

The main lodge, with its piano and library, has a spacious dining room, a convenient bar, and a lounge area tucked neatly into the center of the house. Cocktails, socializing, and parties are held there, often accompanied by Peter's flamenco guitar.

This fishing resort boasts the flawless management and professional expertise most sought after by serious sportsmen, all made possible by Peter McVey, a one-man staff who tries to be all things at once—and succeeds.

As host, Peter displays his
musical attributes by playing
flamenco guitar, entertaining in
the casual setting of the
lounge.

STEAMBOAT INN

Idleyld Park,
Oregon

55

A place that commands extraordinary affection and loyalty.

THE NORTH UMPQUA is known as one of the most difficult North American rivers to fish. Clark Van Fleet, a nature writer and sportsman, devotes an entire chapter of his classic *Steelhead to a Fly* to the North Umpqua. "The roar of its mighty voice fills the canyon of its passage from source to junction as it tumbles down the rough boulder-strewn cleft carved by its journey. A mile of fishing along its banks is a real test of endurance as you snake your way over the folds of bedrock, scramble on jagged reefs, and cross its boulders."

The river is fished by wading. The difficulty comes from the power of the tumultuous white water and from its deceptive nature. To wade the pools where the fish lurk—pools with names like Fighting Hole, Kitchen Pool, Sawtooth, Upper Mott, and Lower Mott—each step must be carefully tested and negotiated. The North Umpqua is also one of the notable rivers for summer-run steelhead, the royalty of Pacific coastal streams. They are largely mature fish, unlike the smaller-sized summer runs of sister rivers, the Eel, the Klamath, and the Rogue.

For fifteen miles in each direction from Steamboat, no bait or spinners are permissible, and only fly-fishing is allowed. No boats are permitted on the river. These conditions create the challenge that brings the most skilled fishermen back, decade after decade.

56

Jim Van Loan's fly-casting form is illustrated on the preceding page. Here he is checking a fly—attending to detail is an essential element of successful fishing.

Fifty feet behind the lodge, this part of the North Umpqua has good trout fishing.

Located on this wonderous Oregon riverway, Steamboat Inn has a long and illustrious history. Constructed of cedar wood and local stones, the structure stands directly on the river. Clarence Gordon, builder of the inn in 1954, knew the river at a time of great fishing, when legends were born of such pioneers as Zane Grey, Zeke Allen, and Major Lawrence Mott.

Tucked serenely by the riverside, Steamboat is an unimaginably peaceful place, and the gentle sound of the river and the frequent rain tapping on the roof adds the dimension of sound to the bliss. While the fishermen and guides are out on the river, the non-fishing guest can sit on the quiet veranda, watching the river in its winding configurations.

58

The main lodge manages to fit half-a-dozen functions into its one big room, but it never appears cramped. A few shelves hold the needed supplies, books, and fishing tackle, and the row of fly rods attached to the cedar-board ceiling merely add the ambience one would expect in a fishing lodge.

Eight guest cabins are set back along a high bank of the river. They are complete with showers, double beds, chests of drawers, linens, and colorful covers much appreciated on the colder nights. In fact, the cabins are situated perfectly, with verandas facing the river and a fortress of Douglas firs behind that traps the river sounds.

Since Jim and Sharon Van Loan took over the operation of the inn, the services have changed. Dinner here is "worth a detour"

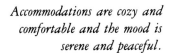

Accommodations are cozy and comfortable and the mood is serene and peaceful.

59

In a striking setting, the inn is sandwiched between the Toketee Route highway and the North Umpqua River.

and is accompanied by strains of Brahms or Beethoven. In the summer it is served a half-hour after dark, and in the winter, about seven o'clock, by reservation only. Guests have automatic reservations.

When all are assembled, the blinds are drawn and a "Closed for the Evening" sign is hung outside. With the outside world removed, the interior is transformed into a night of festivity. Candles are lit. Linen table cloths and colorful napkins bedeck the tables, and silver place settings are arranged with flowers and carafes of wine. Aperitifs before dinner prime appetites.

The dinner bell rings and chef Sharon Van Loan's artistry in the kitchen comes alive as the meal arrives at the one long table. The menu might be Vichyssoise, smoked salmon, a mushroom soufflé and beef Wellington in crusty perfection. Even vegetarian diets are catered to. Coffee and dessert complete the dining experience.

The appeal of the Steamboat Inn's rough-hewn charm is thoroughly intertwined with its owners, the Van Loans, whose motto is "You are a stranger here but once." It is no wonder that the loyalty and affection surrounding this little riverside inn is extraordinary. People have come from around the world, and the guest book, stretching back three decades, is a testimony to the inn.

Dinner is served at sundown—elegantly and intimately.

60

Guest quarters are secluded in the evergreen northwest woods.

HOT

CREEK RANCH

Mammoth Lakes,
California

63

One of our finest and richest dry-fly locations.

O N THE OPEN EXPANSE of a *caldera,* at the foot of Mammoth Mountain in the Sierras, a fisherman delicately removes a barbless hook from the mouth of a handsome brown trout. The fish wriggles in the man's hand as he kneels to release it. Giving the trout a moment to adjust, the angler holds it gently underwater. Then, in a blink, the fish is gone.

At seven thousand feet, and flanked to the west by snow-capped mountain peaks, the eight-mile tributary known as Hot Creek meanders through a grass and sagebrush meadow to a canyon and a sulphur hot springs below. Known the world over as one of America's finest and richest dry fly locations, Hot Creek Ranch is exclusively catch and release, for the wily, stream-spawned brown trout. It is a privately owned facility concerned with maintaining a perfect habitat for wild fish.

64

Windows on the caldera, *your quarters at Hot Creek Ranch.*

Manager Lee Willardson and his dog tend the fishing grounds by trailbike.

In the tradition of British chalk streams, which Hot Creek resembles, Lee Willardson, manager of Hot Creek Ranch, reminds first-timers that only dry flies and barbless hooks are allowed on these pristine waters. Those who wish to fish otherwise must take their nymphs and wet flies downstream to the two-mile, public portion of the creek, which can become quite crowded. Lee explains that a great deal of trouble was taken to introduce the brown trout to the area, and the catch-and-release program insures their continuing availability.

A German by the name of Baron von Behr shipped a batch of brown trout eggs to America in 1883 as a gift to Fred Mather, a writer and fish culturist. Mather gave some to New York State, many to the U.S. Fish Commission in Northville, Michigan, and had the rest distributed throughout America. The brown was introduced to California in 1894 and although it was slow to gain appreciation from the sportsman, because of its difficulty to hook, *Salmo trutta* has now become the most respected member of the trout family. Because it is so wary, the brown survives and attains good size. Two to four pounds is not uncommon, and the record to date in Hot Creek is fourteen and three-quarter pounds.

An excellent specimen of a brown trout, rising on the stream.

There are rainbows and browns in virtually every square foot of the creek. The challenge is to get them to rise.

The cool 58-degree water that the fish flourish in springs from a subterranean source that supports year-round growth of vegetation, which provides an excellent environment for a variety of insects. Aquatic insects are a primary food for wild trout, and Hot Creek teems with caddis flies, May flies, and stone flies in a predictable seasonal pattern. Understanding the life-cycles of these insects is the key to success.

Fifty years ago, Lee Willardson traveled the four hundred miles north of San Diego on a fishing trip and had his first look at the Hot Creek Ranch. Lee couldn't afford the fifty cents charged then for a trespass fee, but he recalls laughingly how he persuaded the rancher to allow him to test the famed waters. His first impressions of it have never faded.

Today Lee Willardson and his wife Rosetta manage the Hot Creek Ranch. Lee says he tries to accommodate everyone. He shares fishing secrets he has acquired over the past half century and predicts when the tiny gray sedges will emerge and start the fish feeding. He suggests tackle and technique, and when it comes to flies, Lee has some simple advice. "Lots of people carry hundreds of flies but you can be successful all season with just two patterns—a gray sedge and a light cahill from Nos. 16 to 20."

In 1966, when the Willardsons assumed the management, the owners built the nine guest cabins from designs Lee drew up. Built of native wood, the cabins are simple yet elegantly modern, and are closely spaced around a one-hundred-year-old structure erected by a Pauite Indian named Tom Poole, who fished and hunted the area.

There is no main lodge here and no central dining facility either, but individual quarters are self-sufficient—clean and well arranged, equipped with full-electric housekeeping facilities and modern

Two miles downstream from the ranch are the famous Hot Creek hot springs, which are wonderful for swimming.

Sunset shows off the ranch's magnificent setting in an extinct volcano.

plumbing. Complete with screened-in-porch, spectacular view, and carport, all a guest need concern himself with is food.

The village at Mammoth Lakes is only eight miles away and offers all the necessary services. Guests are encouraged to shop and dine there. The restaurants are excellent and the arts and crafts are quite extraordinary.

But of all the attractions, one is clearly foremost: the brown trout—the ultimate challenge to the fly fishers' art, and sportsmen are drawn to Hot Creek Ranch as if they were enchanted.

FORK LODGE

Salmon River,
Idaho

Hunting and fishing in rustic splendor.

GETTING TO MIDDLE FORK LODGE is an experience in itself—one that is unforgettable. Because there are no roads, the only way in is by plane, and guests are flown from Boise on the lodge's de Havilland Twin Otter or other aircraft. The plane touches down, after forty minutes, on the gravel runway of Thomas Creek airstrip along the famed Middle Fork of the Salmon River in the heart of the River of No Return Wilderness.

Namah Allen fly fishing on the river in front of the lodge.

Rafting is an exciting sport on the Middle Fork River, and the lodge is a favorite resting spot.

The exciting trip to the lodge is not over! A waiting Land Rover drives guests along the narrow, winding road first crossed by Lewis and Clark in 1805, when they were exploring the Salmon Mountains, which guarded the route to the West. Winding its way to a suspension bridge, the Land Rover traverses the swift Salmon River and drives on to the lodge. A few years ago, the ride to the lodge would have been made in Harrah's antique model T.

Middle Fork Lodge was the deam of Bill Harrah, owner-operator of the famed hotel and casino in Reno, who often entertained well-known performers such as Glenn Campbell, Wayne Newton, and Jim Nabors at the lodge. Although one does not have to be a celebrity to come here, it is one of the most affluent hunting and fishing lodges in America, and boasts heads-of-state among its

74

Western elegance in the River of No Return Wilderness. Meticulous attention to detail is shown at left, above right, and overleaf.

alumnae, including former president Jimmy Carter, who is an ardent angler.

As you come around the bend in the drive, the main building and five cabins appear on the first terrace of a long-extending wave of land that curls around the side of a stepped butte. Sitting quaint and pristine, under the protection of the secluding shade of mammoth cottonwood trees and yellow pine, the ranch is built on three terraces, with a dozen structures meticulous in detail, each of them a tribute to western-style design.

In total harmony with its rugged surroundings, lathe-turned log buildings add to the natural setting, yet all of the modern conveniences are provided for. Guests are accomodated in individual log cabins, upstairs lodging rooms in the main house, or in the River House, typically reserved for honeymooners or those occasional heads of state. All of the rooms are immaculate, and decorated in western motif, highlighted by paintings, sculpture, and prints by noted western artists. Included in the collection are marquetry designs by Namah Allen and works by the American Master, Charles Russell.

Bud Kellow, a long-time employee of Harrah's, runs the lodge. He and Bob Cole, Barbara Hatt, and Namah Allen are your hosts. Bob Cole, Mr. Harrah's personal guide when he was alive, tends to the eighty-acre farm operation at the lodge and the twenty-one horses. He organizes the pack trips, the fishing expeditions, and the hunts. Mr. Cole knows the Idaho back country, and has compiled many photo essays on the flowers, fish, and wild game of the area. All of the employees agree that a day trip into the hills is unrivaled.

Deer, elk, bear, and mountain lion are found here, the latter protected but seen quite often and hunted during the open season along with bighorn sheep and mountain goats, which abound in the area. Seven-day hunts are arranged into the high country for the experienced nimrod. Shorter trips are also available.

For the angler, the Salmon River has a plentiful supply of cutthroat trout, and there is a fully stocked lake on the property.

Expert guide services and equipment are provided for successful hunting and fishing, and the staff is completely up to date on license requirements, bag limits, and all other details. Middle Fork's rule of thumb is two hunters per guide, but for trophy hunting there is one hunter per guide, at an additional charge.

A day of rigorous activities stimulates hearty appetites, and the meals, served ranch-style, are wholesome and completely satisfying. Anything from apple-pecan pancakes in the morning to Shuffman Calypso Creole shrimp in the evening can be found here. Sometimes the kitchen staff is inspired to conjure up something special, like Louisiana chicken, for that state's governor.

At the lodge, guests can shoot billiards, pitch horseshoes, play croquet, or shoot clay pigeons. They can play cards or simply relax on the veranda and by the pool. Patrons of the lodge say in the log book that the photographic opportunities of Idaho's River of No Return Wilderness are "simply unmatched."

Natural hot springs provide the water for the lodge's pool, showers, and baths. A hydro-electric plant supplies the electricity, making the lodge virtually self-sufficient in the Idaho wilderness.

76

CRESCENT

H RANCH

Wilson,
Wyoming

79

Inspired by a love of hunting, fishing, and lodge-style life.

COMBINE WONDERFUL SCENERY, fine accommodations, an experienced staff, and good food with a constant supply of fresh trout in a never-ending selection of well-stocked rivers, and you have the magnet that draws fishermen, environmentalists, and hunters to this wonderful ranch year after year.

Vern Bressler, manager of the Crescent H, has invaluable experience both as a fisherman and a fish biologist. He knows the

At a cookout on the bluffs overlooking the famous Snake River, the cooks do their part with gusto, below, while Cowboy Bob sings and plays old and new Wyoming folk songs, right.

rivers and makes sure the fishing enthusiast has the proper gear and supplies. Necessary arrangements, expert guides, and sack lunches are all looked after, and Vern coordinates everything over the dining room table each evening, while dessert and coffee are served. Questions are always encouraged and important fishing information is shared.

The ranch offers cutthroat, rainbow, and brown trout fishing in rivers that include the Snake, Green, Yellowstone, New Fork, and Salt. The rivers are fished on a day-trip basis. Crescent H has its own stream and three smaller spring creeks identified only by numbers One, Two, and Three.

June and July are the times for the big dry flies and nymphs. Early summer temperatures bring huge hatches of stoneflies to the river's surface. Along with them come the voraciously feeding trout, followed by the avid fishermen hoping for the best fly fishing of the year. Using dry flies, one can expect a large cutthroat or brown. With a personal guide and five miles of private rivers and streams to wade in, Crescent H offers the fisherman some of the best trout fishing in the West.

The ultimate in classic western living.

82

Built in 1928 by a fishing enthusiast, the ranch's inception was inspired by a love of hunting and fishing and the excitement of lodge-style life. The grand dining hall reflects that spirit—a bull moose peering down from the twelve-foot mark on the wall—but combined with the trappings of civilization, like sterling silver, and bronze sculptures. Stone fireplaces dominate the log walls at both ends of the room, and the ceiling is open to the roof, with criss-crossing log support beams. On one side, there are wagon-wheel coffee tables, paintings of the Old West, fat-pillowed couches, and antique pieces of furniture, cabinets, and rugs. The same traditional and rustic decor is found in the guest quarters, which consist of log cabins with modern showers and marble-topped bedside tables. Baskets of fresh fruit await new guests.

The grounds around the property were used as a TV location for the CBS production of Earl Hammer's *A Homecoming; A Christmas Story*. Because big game abounds near here, the lodge has many mounted tags on display. Behind the ranchhouse, horseback riders scaling the mountain can encounter moose, bear, antelope or deer. Vern's son, Joe Bressler, is known all over Wyoming as a gifted

Kenny Hastings, assistant manager, coaches a beginner in the techniques of fly casting.

83

hunting guide, and he is eagerly sought after for his skill in stalking game.

Evenings at the ranch provide hunting revelations of the past. Over a campfire, Cowboy Bob strums his guitar and tells stories of the open range. Laughter abounds and the music casts a spell of serenity. The setting is enchanting, with its clear, bright, galaxy-filled sky and, below, the Snake River curving powerfully through the countryside. An Alpine road trails out of sight into hills covered in purple grasses and yellow daisies. Beyond are the mountains. Purple-pink at dawn and slate-blue at dusk, these sometimes misty, craggy, cloud-high peaks thrust abruptly from the floor of Jackson Hole into the wide Wyoming sky. Majestic by day, mysterious by night, the Grand Tetons hover over this great land.

Whether you plan a five-day fishing vacation or a week's enrollment in the fly-fishing school at Crescent H, the available activities include services for float trips, canoeing, sailing, horseback riding, hiking, and wildlife photography. Everything from shotgun shooting to just plain relaxing is available at this lodge.

84

The ranch's rivers, streams, and meadows provide the settings; the guests do the rest.

MABEL'S ISLAND

Lake-of-the-Woods,
Ontario

A private retreat for families who hunt and fish together.

ONE OF FOURTEEN THOUSAND ISLANDS stretching across a glacial labyrinth, Mabel's Island is the private retreat of Doug Kenyon, a wealthy Chicago businessman. Here, in Lake-of-the-Woods, Ontario, amid primordial forests and crystal-clear lakes, the wilderness is celebrated with style.

Built in 1929 by Charles Kratsch, an executive of the Maytag Company, and purchased by Kenyon six years ago, the lodge provides both comfort and elegance. A forty-foot flag pole, flying Canadian and American flags, a three-slip boat house, and a screened gazebo all enhance the wonderful log retreat where leading sportsmen and dignitaries have hunted and fished while living in the grand manner.

The house is furnished in classic lodge furnishings of exceptional quality. Audubon prints, mounted birds, a rack of antlers, firearms, carved animal night lamps, and a prize white polar bear rug embellish the furniture in the central room, with its peaked, log ceiling. Personal touches reveal Kenyon for the sportsman of distinction he is. A Moosehead over the living room fireplace is a trophy he brought back from the Brooks Range in Alaska. The thirteen-hundred-and-

On the previous page, Doug Kenyon and his daughter, Chris, demonstrate the art of relaxing, down at the boathouse. At right, Chris and her mother, Linda, demonstrate the art of fishing.

No expense was spared in building this very special log fishing lodge.

88

fifty-pound moose was felled by a single shot. A mounted eighteen-pound Arctic char was caught on the Tree River in the Canadian Arctic.

Doug Kenyon is an experienced guide. Once employed as a guide in Yellowstone, he has also explored far-reaching parts of Alaska and the Canadian North. Here, in Lake-of-the-Woods, his knowledge of the water and its exceptional fishing is uncanny.

At the lodge, he offers an exclusive experience to parties of four or five, preferably a family compatible with his own, who will be treated as his personal guests.

Kenyon will be at his guests' disposal. Fishing can be arranged at dawn, in the afternoon, into dusk and beyond, according to individual lifestyles. Musky, northern pike, smallmouth bass, lake trout, and walleye are all fished here. The duck shooting is exceptional, and deer are plentiful. Camera outings and wilderness jaunts, swimming, water skiing, and afternoon cocktails round out the good life the Kenyons offer.

Not to be taken lightly is Linda Kenyon's cooking, which she prepares for guests at the lodge. The kitchen seethes with the aroma of tantalizing stews, delicately flavored fish, garden vegetables in broth, and home-baked breads and pastries. She is the perfect hostess to complement Doug's expertise as a guide.

An entry in a log book made by Mr. Kratsch in 1935 captures the Kenyons' feeling about Mabel's Island. "As I look back down the years, the bright spots along the way, which represent those happy periods of pleasure spent in the woods and along the streams, or in the blinds in marsh or field, are filled with the faces of the congenial friends who chose me for a partner. The memory of their companionship is what proves that it is not the game we kill or the fish we catch that endures . . . . It is the tie of understanding friendship between us and our companions of the chase that makes the sport worthwhile."

90

The interiors of a classic hunting and fishing lodge are augmented by the personal art collection of the Kenyons.

FORTEAU

SALMON LODGE

L'Anse au Clair,
Labrador

Thrills and grandeur on Labrador's frontier.

THE THRILL OF SALMON FISHING on Labrador's primeval lakes and rivers is matched only by the grandeur of the surrounding landscape. Huge lichen-covered mountains of stone stand sentinel over moor-like swales cloaked in dwarf pine and spotted with treacherous peat bogs, brittle-as-coral caribou moss, spongy orange moss, and moss as green and lush as velvet. Masses of edible wild berries in shades of indigo, cream, carnelian, and topaz add brilliant color to the prospect and delicacies to the table. Swift, inky rivers cascade over ancient rock and flow into the cold waters of the Strait of Belle Isle, which is lined with broad expanses of sandy beach. Eight tiny fishing villages, tucked into sheltering coves and populated by just over two thousand souls make up the Straits of Labrador. Labradorians love their land fiercely and cleave to it as closely as the lichen to rock. And so, besides great fishing, the Forteau Salmon Lodge provides an excuse to visit this gateway to the end of the world.

The lodge sits high on the banks of the Forteau River at the place where it empties into the Strait of Belle Isle. The building is rudimentary and similar in style to the majority of structures along the coast. Inside, an enclosed veranda runs the length of the building. Six private bedrooms, an ample kitchen and dining area, and a lounge comprise the rest of the lodge. Soon to be completed is a large screened-in porch that will overlook the river and where meals will be served. Owners Steve and Shirley Letto are natives of Labrador and also own the only large motel complex in the

94

Typical Labrador architecture in L'Anse au Clair.

Owner Steve Letto, a Labrador native.

Straits, in the village of L'Anse au Clair. They bring to the lodge the hospitality of experienced innkeepers, Labrador-style.

Needless to say, fishing the Labrador frontier can be superb, with salmon ranging in size from four to twenty-two pounds. The final three miles of the Forteau River is like a necklace; it is made up of a series of large ponds connected by a wide ribbon of water. One of the most popular and fruitful spots is Ladies' Pool, which is a fast-flowing stretch between the first and second ponds, a stretch that is fed by a dramatic graduated waterfall. Until high water in August enables the salmon to scale the powerful falls, the fish are held back in the various pools, which makes for highly rewarding sport. The Pinware River, several miles north of the lodge, is another angler's dream. As it happens, if the fish aren't rising in the Forteau they usually can be caught in the Pinware, and vice versa. And so, depending on the whim of the fish, you may journey to this wild river.

Besides salmon, the pools of the Forteau are filled with brook

The boat station and guide Bill Flynn at Ladies' Pool, seen from the ground.

Excellent fly-casting form is shown by John Walker of Guelph, Ontario.

*Ladies' Pool on
the Forteau River,
seen from the air.*

trout which range in size anywhere from one-half pound to five pounds. Some of the largest brook trout in North America have been captured in the inland waters of Labrador. A few of these ponds are accessible by boat and foot but the best are reached by float plane. Therefore, fishing these back waters is offered by the lodge, "weather permitting."

The weather in Labrador is totally unpredictable and visitors should pack accordingly. The bane of the summer season is the ubiquitous blackfly, which is in its prime during the height of the salmon season. Liberal application of a strong repellent wards off this pesky creature.

Food at the lodge is plentiful but is somewhat limited in scope, due to a short growing season and isolation from rich agricultural areas. However, in a typical week you'll happily devour lobster, stuffed pork chops, steak, baked ham, and, of course, a fisherman's platter that includes cod tongues, cod au gratin, and poached salmon. The bakeapple, which is an orange berry of the raspberry family and the pride of Labrador, is a tangy fruit served in parfaits and pies.

WADE'S

FISHING LODGE

Blackville,
New Brunswick

Atlantic salmon on the famous Miramichi.

ARLY IN THIS CENTURY a sportsman and outfitter named Harry Allen pioneered the waterways of central New Brunswick, Canada, and eventually took his nephew Charles Wade on as a guide. For many years Wade escorted fishing parties along the chain of rivers, canoeing and camping along the banks of these beautiful reaches. When Allen died in 1933, Wade bought twelve acres of land just below the confluence of the Cains and Miramichi Rivers and founded Wade's Fishing Lodge. As the father and the uncle before him, Charles' son, Herb, was drawn to the river, and he helped his father create a comfortable home for visiting sportsmen. He also caught some fair-sized salmon along the way and was the Provincial fly-casting champion each year that New Brunswick sponsored a tournament.

Three generations of love for the Miramichi have gone into Wade's Fishing Lodge and you can feel it. It is much the same

Individual cabins look out on the Miramichi.

100

Comfortable, rustic cabin interiors create a warm glow most welcome in the North Woods.

The wonderful aroma of freshly baked bread and pastries pervades the morning air each day.

here today as it was in 1933. The camp sits on a hill that rises high above the river and is shrouded by towering pines and white birch. The original cabin that Charles and Herb built now houses the dining room, kitchen, and lounge. In the lounge many black-and-white photographs, memories of days gone by, hang on the walls and others fill two photo albums. Two mounted salmon speak better than words of the Miramichi's potential for trophy fish. The entire room, from its full timber beams and walls to the old-fashioned cabinet radio and blazing fire, is warm and relaxing. Three large guest cabins, an office with extra bedrooms, bunkhouses for the guides and lodge staff, an immaculate room for cleaning fish, and a walk-in cooler for storing your catch make up the remainder of Wade's compound.

No matter how generous a river may be, there is always a day, even a week, when salmon won't cooperate. There are years of plenty and years of scarcity on the best rivers in the world. This frustration can ruin what might have been a great vacation. But with Dorothy McCormack installed in the kitchen, Herb Wade outsmarts both the elements and the fish. Dorothy has been baking since she was fourteen years old and she's been the cook at Wade's since 1961. No matter the weather or mood of the salmon, Dorothy's good cooking keeps everyone in high spirits. She specializes in baked goods and the loaves of bread she pulls out of the oven are puffed so high and golden they must be seen to be believed. The supply of fresh doughnuts, cakes, and cookies, not to mention light-as-air biscuits and perfect pancakes, is abundant. To gild the lily, a piece of Dorothy's delectable pie is offered at the end of the afternoon and evening meals. In addition to these guilt-making goodies Dorothy concocts flavorful soups, cooks salmon to perfection, and grills a steak precisely as ordered. Regulars at Wade's watch for the appearance of Dorothy's salmon chowder and biscuits and pounce on them so eagerly you'd think they hadn't eaten in days.

102

*Head guide Jimmy Coffey
instructs his pupil,
author Roberta Gardner,
in the fine art of fly casting,
left, above. A rod, reel
and beautiful set of
wet flies are shown below.*

*A fishing lesson
in process on the lush
green shores of
the Miramichi.*

Besides eating, a bit of fishing fills the hours at Wade's. To say that the Miramichi is one of the world's great salmon rivers is an understatement. As Herb says, "More Atlantic salmon are taken here than any other place on the North American continent." Each year the Miramichi bears a heavy run of grilse, but the adult salmon can run up to thirty pounds or more.

Each fisherman at Wade's is given a boat and a guide, and these guides know the rivers like the backs of their hands. Head guide Jimmy Coffey is Dorothy McCormack's brother and he brings to his job expertise and easy-going good humor. In fact, most of the guides are related to Jimmy and Dorothy either by blood or by marriage, which makes for a close family atmosphere—an atmosphere that attracts a wide and loyal following.

104

More expert fly casting is done on the Miramichi than on most rivers of North America. Above is James T. Grey, Jr. of Yardley, Pennsylvania, who has written the definitive book on salmon fishing on the Margaree River. Below is Canadian Tony Ray of Antigonish, Nova Scotia.

Lodge owner Herb Wade fly casting.

LEEN'S LODGE

Grand Lake Stream,
Maine

"The Waldorf of the Wilderness."

LEEN'S LODGE in Grand Lake Stream, Maine, satisfies both experienced anglers and first-time fishermen alike—and everyone in between! This impressive accomplishment is achieved by combining high quality lakes and streams with comfortable accommodations, great food, and the impeccable hospitality of owner Stanley Leen.

Grand Lake, located in the dense woodlands of northeastern Maine, is the largest lake in a network of waters offering typical Down East angling. The feisty smallmouth bass, lake trout or togue, white perch, and pickerel are abundant. One of the country's oldest salmon hatcheries is situated on the banks of Grand Lake Stream, which makes for excellent landlocked salmon fishing. Besides good fishing, twenty-mile-long West Grand Lake itself is spectacular. The water is startlingly clear and the lake is dotted with glacial granite boulders and tiny islands.

The lodge encompasses a small peninsula, which gives guests a feeling of island privacy. Rustic cabins are scattered along the shoreline and each has a fireplace or Franklin stove, living room, picture windows, a refrigerator, and comfortable beds. Though similar in design, each has its own individual character.

Morning begins with a hearty breakfast, which might include the cook's special Maine blueberry griddlecakes and sausage. If you choose to go fishing with a guide, your man will be waiting for you after breakfast. Over two dozen experienced guides live in and around the area and, besides knowing the waters well, they distinguish themselves in two unique ways. First, they use Grand Lake

Still later, the Tannery Room all lit up for its important activities.

On the previous page lodge owner Stanley Leen enjoying the view of Grand Lake with author Roberta Gardner. Left is another view of Grand Lake somewhat later, at sunset.

108

Diving from the boat houses in the hamlet of Grand Lake Stream.

Individual lodges overlook the lake, amid the fresh smells of the forest.

canoes, which are built right in the town of Grand Lake Stream. It is a pleasure to glide through the water in one of these handsome and well-crafted boats. Second, guide service includes an expertly prepared shore lunch. Each guide carries an iron skillet, large coffeepot, and the gear needed to produce a satisfying repast. The lodge kitchen will pack a lunch, which can include sandwiches, chicken, steak, beverages, and dessert. You, then, provide your morning's catch for a luncheon tidbit or satisfying main course. You'll also learn the Maine guide method for preparing coffee, complete with whole egg!

If you don't choose to fish you can spend the day swimming and sunning on the sand beach or on the sturdy float anchored close to shore. Or you might hike along a well-marked trail to the fire tower, which offers a panoramic view of the territory, and then on to the village where you'll discover the well-stocked general store, the salmon hatchery, and a rustic wooden dam.

Leen's is the perfect place for families. It is Stan Leen's belief that people who have good experiences in this type of natural setting early in life are hooked for life. Therefore, Leen's welcomes children and offers them both freedom and responsibility. Besides fishing, swimming, hiking, ping pong, and shuffleboard, children can try their hands at the lodge's sailfish, canoes, or motorboat. The area is so private and well-planned that none of this activity disturbs the prevailing calm.

After a long day filled with activity or lazing about, you can enjoy a leisurely conversation in the Tannery Room, which contains books and magazines, a bar, television, and is filled with interesting artifacts from the days when Grand Lake Stream natives made their living in the fur tanning trade. Then on to dinner where you'll tuck into a generous steak, Maine Lobster, New England corned beef dinner, leg of lamb, pot roast, or one of the other delicious dishes served up from the kitchen.

There is a great spirit of comfort and hospitality at Leen's Lodge for which Stan Leen is responsible. As he says with a chuckle, "I used to call this place 'The Waldorf of the Wilderness.' We dropped that title—didn't want to make them mad—but we still do everything in our power to see that people get what they want. If you like the outdoors and lakes and woods, we've got it."

Fighting a smallmouth bass.

Guide Don Howe in one of the special canoes, made locally.

Author Gardner with a proud string of smallmouth bass.

113

Shore lunch time.

GARNET

HILL LODGE

North River,
New York

One of the finest lodges in the Adirondacks.

T HE IROQUOIS CONFEDERATION called the Adirondacks "the dark and bloody land," too wild to civilize and suitable only for warfare, hunting, and little else. Since that time, twentieth-century technology and population booms have made few inroads. To this day the Adirondacks remain 5,000 square miles of virtual wilderness crossed by one north-south highway and two roads running east and west. Hunting these parts has always presented an exciting challenge, with whitetail deer being the most sought-after game. Only the hardiest deer survive this rugged environment, which accounts for the high percentage of trophy bucks taken each year. Fisherman also flock to the area for the brook, brown, and rainbow trout, landlocked salmon, bass, and pike that are caught in abundance in the network of ponds, rivers, and streams that thread through mountain valleys.

One of the finest lodges in the Adirondacks is located along a dirt road at the gateway to the 50,000-acre Siamese Ponds Wilderness Area. Garnet Hill Lodge exists in stark contrast to its wild environment. Comprised of a main lodge, dubbed Log House, a secondary manse named Big Shanty, and a series of out-cabins, tennis courts, cross-country ski facilities, and twenty-five miles of well-tended trails, this rustic compound attracts hunters and fishermen as well as hikers, honeymooners, and nature lovers. Owned and operated by George and Mary Heim, Garnet Hill exudes a spirit of warmth, simplicity, and total relaxation.

Not the least of Garnet Hill's charms is the cooking of Mary

116

There are several buildings in use on the property—all with names. On the previous page is the beautiful lounge and library at Big Shanty, where sportsmen stay. At right is Log House, which is the general center of activity.

Owner George Heim in the autumn sun.

Heim. She sets a fine table, preparing simple feasts with a sensitive touch. Mary roasts beef to pink perfection, imparts a buttery essence to lightly breaded chicken breasts, and elevates the common meat-loaf or ham casserole to haute cuisine. Her homemade soups, such as turkey and wild rice, are legendary. Hot muffins appear each morning, though you might choose to forgo them to save room for light, fluffy flapjacks with pure maple syrup or golden French toast made from thick slices of homemade bread. Each evening a different variety of fresh-baked bread makes its tempting appearance and desserts are irresistible. Favorites include banana cream, blueberry, or apple pie nestled in a rich flaky crust, chewy chocolate brownies topped with ice cream and a chocolate sauce, or a simple plate of crisp oatmeal cookies bedecked with walnuts and coconut.

Returning to the lodge for lunch in a pickup after a morning's deer hunting.

Black powder hunter Victor Sasse, who runs a sporting goods store in North River. He is holding a .50 caliber Thompson Center Muzzleloader.

he lounge
t Log House.

Both the Log House and Big Shanty are dominated by two giant garnet stone fireplaces—chunks of the shiny red mineral, mined in the surrounding hills, sparkle brightly in the light of flickering fires. The walls and ceiling of Log House are full- and half-timbers with thick, burnished tree-trunk columns supporting the second-floor guestrooms. Everyone gathers in this classic lodge for meals and to enjoy a spectacular view of 13th Lake at the base of Garnet Hill. During hunting season, or if a group of fishermen book a stay, Big Shanty acts as sportsmen's headquarters. Besides the immense garnet fireplace, walls are lined—floor to ceiling—with books, a moosehead hanging over the hearth observes comings and goings, and intricate diamond-paned windows cast light about the birchbark beams and columns.

Because the Adirondack wilderness poses a formidable challenge, those hunting with a qualified local guide reap the greatest rewards. While many hunters are content to stay close to civilization, the bulk of the whitetail populate more obscure areas and so the odds of taking a trophy while hunting well-beaten paths are slim. The same holds true with success in fishing. Guides familiar with the terrain go where the fish are. And while no guide service works out of Garnet Hill, George Heim sees to it that all interested parties are set up with the best in that area. The peak fishing period on 13th Lake is right after ice-out in late April, when landlocked salmon and brook trout are feeding on the surface. However, the nearby Hudson River headwaters section is noted for its excellent trout fishing throughout the season; this is dominantly brown trout water, but rainbows, brook trout, and some landlocked salmon are present also.

120

View of 13th Lake from hiking trail, with Jenny the dog.

Big Shanty from the outside.

BURNT PINE

PLANTATION

Madison,
Georgia

123

Superb hunting, thanks to proper land management.

IN THE 1800s, the thick hedgerows and stands of pine that lined plantation cotton fields provided the perfect habitat for the bobwhite quail and the whitetail deer, and there was no finer place in the world to hunt than the state of Georgia. In those days the numbers of quail seemed endless and the gentlemanly sport of bird hunting became an art form. But over the years, as the plantation was transformed into large and highly mechanized farms, the hedgerow disappeared and the pine grew into dense forests. These combined factors took their toll and Georgia's native wildlife—most particularly the endemic quail—dramatically diminished in number.

In the 1970s, avid sportsman David Morris recognized the source of the problems plaguing Georgia's wildlife and set about to return 14,000 acres of gentle and rolling countryside to that earlier happy state. At Burnt Pine Plantation, Mr. Morris is proving that proper land management makes for superb hunting.

Woodland and field management has recreated the same ideal quail habitat of years gone by.

On the previous page is one of a variety of tree stands for sighting deer. Below, the dogs at Burnt Pine play an important role in raising quail hunting there to an art form.

124

Keith Odon, in foreground, and David Griffith exhibit the good form in hunting bobwhite quail that dates back to plantation life.

A group of hunters sighting their guns on the shooting range before the hunt.

Archery has its own season at Burnt Pine as an alternate form of deer hunting.

Deer hunting at Burnt Pine is second to none. An extraordinarily large number of trophy bucks, many scoring high on the Boone and Crockett records, are taken at Burnt Pine each year. In part, this is due to the fact that the deer population is made up of direct descendants of the Wisconsin and Texas "big bucks" that were imported into Georgia in the 1950s. In addition, Burnt Pine employs full-time land managers who keep a sharp eye on genetics and apply strenuous environmental measures to the land, culling as many spike horn bucks as possible, burning back thousands of acres of timberland each year to allow wild food crops to grow, and planting hundreds of acres of nutritious grains to be consumed solely by grazing herds of deer. Choosing to cultivate high quality rather than high quantity deer, the plantation staff promotes the practice of hunters seeking the best specimen before taking a shot. They tell many stories of hunters who have taken eight- to twelve-point deer after passing up the six-pointer that passed by their stand minutes earlier.

The stringent land management program that provides good nutrition and shelter for deer is equally beneficial to the bobwhite quail. Though quail are just beginning to stage a comeback and thus are seldom hunted, the plantation stocks a great number of high-quality, flight-conditioned birds. Burnt Pine offers hunters great shooting and an opportunity to work with topnotch guides and watch fine bird dogs in action. The dogs at Burnt Pine are well trained and observing them as they back each other and point in field trial style can be as satisfying as the shoot itself. During the height of the season, when all hands are occupied with the serious business of stalking deer, hunters can take time to fish for bass and bluegill in any one of the plantation's fifteen beautiful ponds.

The lodge consists of a modest brick ranch-style house and two separate bunk houses. In the main house hunters gather in the living room, in front of the roaring fire, to swap stories and share a relaxing drink before dinner, or simply to enjoy the aroma of good Southern cooking as it wafts from the kitchen. Three satisfying meals materialize each day, with golden, juicy quail, channel catfish caught right on the property, fried chicken, and country ham as the house specialties.

Burnt Pine Plantation prides itself on its casual, low-key atmosphere. Says David Morse, "When we were getting started we had to decide whether to adopt a formal atmosphere, which would have included dressing for dinner and a certain regimentation. But that seemed to be what most people want to get away from. So we decided on a slow and easy pace with strict attention to service. And, of course, very good hunting."

Burnt Pine admirably achieves its goals.

Guide Colonel Gerald Graham, right, was the top aide to General Douglas MacArthur, and is a great story teller.

Dee Wilbanks of Talking Rock, Georgia, happily displays his 8 point, 3½-year-old, 200-pound buck.

128

The lounge, where hunters gather in anticipation of good southern cooking.

TELICO
JUNCTION

HUNTING PRE-
SERVE

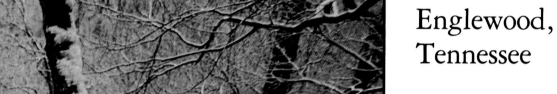

Englewood,
Tennessee

Hunting wild boar is the exotic specialty.

LEGIONS OF BRILLIANT PEACOCKS, parading and preening across the lawn, provide a colorful welcome to the Telico Junction Hunting Preserve in the Great Smoky Mountains of Tennessee. Noted primarily for an abundance of exotic wild boar and for the beauty and rugged challenge of its thousand acres, this preserve also offers hunters a chance to stalk the rare Mauna Kea sheep, wild turkey, Spanish goat, barbedow sheep, and fallow, or sika, deer.

Wild boar, for which the preserve has made its name, is not native to the United States. It was imported into the country in 1910 by a businessman named George Moore when he established a large game preserve in the mountains along the North Carolina and Tennessee border. His primary motive for doing this was to entertain potential European investors, and to this end he brought in ten wild European sows and three boars from Germany, which were reputed to be members of the fierce Prussian breed. When the herd grew to a size large enough to provide a full-fledged hunt, Moore invited his affluent friends to the first boar hunt in the U.S. In a comedy of errors, only two boar were bagged, many hunters suffered injury or stark terror, and a large number of the boar broke down the wooden fence that penned them in and escaped into the wilderness. These boar eventually mated with free-range Southern razorback hogs that had become feral and the mountains soon were full of this hybrid, which was the first true American wild boar.

132

The spring-fed ponds and the mountain-style lodge buildings are the focus of the thousand-acre preserve.

Owner Joe Meeks and his favorite dog.

Telico Junction is known for its peacocks, which decorate the grounds and frighten the cats.

Thousands of acres of wilderness surround the Telico Junction Preserve and it is here that the descendants of those first wild boar are nurtured. In fact, this area has been called "the main bastion of the European wild boar in America." The boar that roam the preserve are trapped in the wild by owner Joe Meeks and then released into his fenced acreage. The animals vary in size and coloration, some resembling their European parents, with dark skin, high, thick shoulders, and prominent, razor-sharp tusks, while others seem closer to what we know as their domestic relatives. But they are all unpredictable, and very wild. In fact, it is in this volatile temperament that the challenge lies. According to Joe, "Boar can be *very* ornery. They don't all charge you, but you never know which one will charge. I've been chased up a tree lots of times but my record was made the day I was treed eleven times by three different hogs. They are very tough animals and

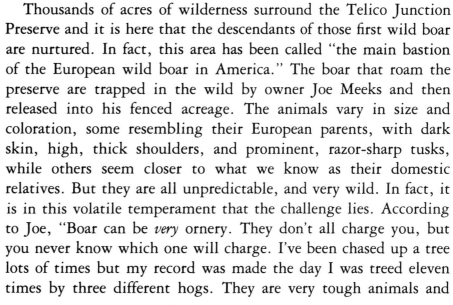

Scenting the boar at the start of the hunt.

The prize: a trophy wild boar, still looking fierce.

The dogs have caught up with a boar, who might either become confused by the harrying, or become a dangerous attacker.

135

This hunter used a pistol to get his boar.

can fight to their last breath, even after taking lots of lead." Joe has the scars to prove his stories.

Each hunt is tailored to the individual hunter. The terrain is extremely rough, with endless steep climbs and perilous precipices, and the strength and endurance of the most stalwart hunter can be tested. But by using Joe's four-wheel-drive vehicles and well-trained dogs a satisfying hunt can be had by each and every hunter, no matter what their physical condition. Joe even guarantees a kill to all hunters who use a standard deer hunting rifle, though bows, muzzle loaders, pistols, and shotguns are permitted. Accommodations at the preserve include two comfortable, clean, and spacious trailers with fully equipped kitchens, charcoal grills, picnic tables, and television, as well as one small mountain-style house that

Trophy Tom turkey hunters are, from left to right, Larry Becker, from New Jersey, Charles McCann, from New York, and Tom Stellato, from New Jersey.

contains two well-furnished apartments. Although meals are not supplied, Joe and his wife Mazie direct their guests to the best restaurants nearby.

Flush with the wooded ridge that creates a dramatic back-drop for the lodge are three spring-fed ponds where anglers can while away the hours or swimmers can take a dip. You can also tour the preserve's taxidermy studio, which employs several masters of the craft and enjoys a reputation for high quality workmanship. You may choose to leave your trophy to be mounted and have all the edible meat expertly packaged in the Meekses' butcher shop, which is also on the property. When you realize the wealth of wild game available at this preserve, you may want to mount more than one fine trophy.

THE ISLANDS

Marco,
Florida

A grand oasis of luxury and sport in the Everglades.

Overhead view that illustrates the perfect symmetry of the main lounge.

To MOST OF US, mention of the Florida Everglades conjures up visions of hot, wet, impenetrable jungle, a no man's land filled with alligators and snakes and mosquitos. Port of the Islands resort, twenty-two miles southeast of Naples, Florida, and in the center of this delicately balanced wilderness, dispels that image and puts it to rest forever. This is a grand oasis of luxury rising out of nowhere—which means from sawgrass and cypress swamp and a forest of mangrove known as the

On the previous page is Tony Renkert, chief guide at the lodge, who knows the Ten Thousand Islands better than anyone.

The main lodge of the Bayside part of the complex, showing the formality of the Spanish architectural style.

140

Ten Thousand Islands. These myriad islands choke the coast between Marco Island and Everglades City and create bays and rivers that provide shelter for a variety of gamefish.

The Port of the Islands complex is made up of two separate resorts that are bisected by the Tamiami Trail. On the Bayside of the highway an imposing main hotel building and series of motel units surround a hibiscus and palm-shaded swimming pool and face onto the marina. A second massive hotel complex is located on the Riverside and contains yet another swimming pool, impressive dioramas depicting the three major environments of the area, a recreational vehicle park, and a skeet and trap range, with an Olympic running boar range as well, which is managed by world champion trap and skeet shooter, Russ Howard. On both sides, Moorish arched alcoves and red-tile roofs, ceiling paddle fans, giant plants potted in terra cotta, bamboo furniture, and glistening floor tiles create a cool and tropical atmosphere. Besides the mandatory swimming pools, Port of the Islands is outfitted with six top-notch tennis courts, shuffleboard, day bars and nightclubs, a fully equipped marina, and a 3500-foot landing strip for private aircraft. Both hotels have full-service restaurants though Bayside has been in operation longer and is better established. A sophisticated and delicious

Dressed in red, Russ Howard, world champion trap and skeet shooter, supervises the shooting range.

Tony Renkert helps land a prize sheepshead fish.

View of Bayside from the waterway leading to the Ten Thousand Islands.

142

selection of appetizers, entrées, and desserts is available, ranging from escargot and oysters Rockefeller to quail and rack of lamb, and perhaps Key lime pie or a pecan ball drenched in fudge sauce to finish. The kitchen also features a "Maine Lobster and seafood extravaganza" during the week and a generous Sunday brunch. These are delectable affairs that attract a faithful local following.

That the resort has access to one of the finest snook habitats in Florida is just the tip of the angling iceberg. Offering some of the best fishing in the state, these waters are home to tarpon, redfish, snapper, flounder, sea trout, black grouper, and sheepshead. In October, Port of the Islands sponsors a hugely popular redfish tournament that includes festive meals, cocktail parties, and ceremonial awards for the winners.

To successfully negotiate the confusing maze of mangrove islands that grow thick along the coast, a guide is mandatory. Though many competent guides work out of the marina, if you're lucky you'll hook up with the master in residence, Tony Renkert. He and his wife Jo, who works in the marina, live aboard a boat docked at Port of the Islands. Tony looks the part of the "old salt," with full white beard and permanent saltwater tan, and he knows these islands better than anyone. The marina is stocked with all the bait and

Another view of the wonderful main lounge at Bayside.

144

Tony Renkert performing the dockside ritual of cleaning and fileting the day's catch.

145

The perfect end of a perfect day at Port of the Islands.

tackle you might need, though most visitors bring their own light tackle.

Besides fishing, simply being located in the center of a unique natural habitat makes Port of the Islands worth a visit. Manatee roll sluggishly in the channel, watched over by cormorants and pelicans that stand sentinel on every available marker. Porpoise and stingray, osprey, blue heron, and wood ibis are abundant, and, if you are sharp-sighted, you may spot the occasional bald eagle, sandhill crane, or roseate spoonbill. The area is also full of interesting side trips, including Corkscrew Swamp with its giant ferns, tree snails, orchids, wildlife; the clean, white beaches of Marco Island; and airboat rides and swamp buggy rides through the Everglades.

CHEECA LODGE

Islamorada,
Florida Keys

"Sportfishing Capital of the World."

A T FIRST GLANCE, Cheeca Lodge appears to be no more than an exclusive resort catering to sophisticated sun worshippers, tennis buffs, and golfers. One block off busy Highway 1 on Islamorada in the Florida Keys, visitors enter Cheeca and come upon an executive golf course—a Jack Nicklaus design suggested for the spot by Nicklaus himself, a frequent guest. Four tennis courts border the pool that, in turn, leads to an enclosed snack bar/game parlor for teenagers and a complete playground for tots. Two Jacuzzis and an exercise room are hidden amidst the enshrouding greenery. Comfortable accommodations occupy the top floors of the lodge and a row of villas and cottages meander along the beach. The first hint of Cheeca's raison d'être is found in the lodge where pecky cypress walls are resplendent with tackle and trophy fish; the management's love of sky and water is

Notable food elegantly served in a resort setting.

The real lure of the lodge is fishing for tarpon, bonefish, sailfish, and marlin.

reflected in a marine blue and sparkling white decor. At shoreline a pier juts 525-feet into the Atlantic Ocean and is equipped with benches, running water, night lights, and a partial roof for protection from the elements. Thatched cabañas and comfortable lounge chairs complete the beach scene, which is in clear view from the glassed-in dining room. The chef is, by any measure, three stars, and serves some of the best food in the state. Dining at Cheeca on native lobster, snapper, grouper, and prime cuts of meat, hot sourdough rolls, and savory soups, crisp salads, and desserts is sheer delight. But as diverting as all this is, the real reason for Cheeca's celebrated existence is Carl Navarré's consuming passion for sport fishing.

Navarré began fishing the Caribbean in 1946 and discovered Islamorada quite by accident when a storm blew him far away from his destination, Bimini, and into the island's sheltering harbor. The joys of fishing for tarpon, bonefish, and permit in the colorful waters of Florida Bay soon became apparent and he was hooked. In 1976 he purchased an almost abandoned hotel that was on the road to ruin. Months of unceasing labor reclaimed Cheeca from the clutch of the jungle and over the years the lodge has been transformed and refined into today's plush resort.

While fishing of all kinds is an everyday thing at Cheeca, annual tournaments for shark and sailfish as well as the speedy bonefish and acrobatic tarpon are by now legendary. Several of the invitationals—most particularly the Islamorada Invitational Tarpon Fly Championship—are exclusive and pricey affairs that test the mettle of world-class sportsmen and give credence to Islamorada's self-

150

Jack Nicklaus designed the golf course that adjoins the lodge.

The lodge's private promenade dock.

*The popular bar
near the lodge
where guests and locals
compare stories and
watch the pelicans.*

proclaimed title of "Sportfishing Capital of the World." But, of
course, one need not be a pro to enjoy the fishing here. Cheeca
awards citations for fish of a qualifying size and a Hall of Fame
plaque in the Trophy Room lists names for prize catches. Snook
and redfish are prime in the winter and provide nocturnal diversion
when fishing off the pier after dark, if one must fish after dark.

Islamorada guides are notorious perfectionists, but they are
undeniably knowledgable. Carl Navarré says, "Teamwork is involved,
and a fisherman and his guide will either become fast friends or
total strangers." Another writer has recorded that "all the money
in the world won't put you out of range, should you deserve it, of
the sharp tongues of the guides at Islamorada, who form an aris-
tocracy of their own." Forewarned is forearmed.

The congenial atmosphere of Islamorada is owed in great part to
its proximity to the sparkling turquoise and lime-green water, dark
turtle-grass flats, and deep-green mangrove islands of the Bay. And
Cheeca is a special haven because it offers layers of diversions, luxuries, and comforts.

CLUB DE PATOS

Sisal,
Yucatan

153

A Yucatan haven ideal for duck hunting.

A T FIRST GLANCE, card-carrying gringos might well suffer a pang of wonder at what they've gotten themselves into. Driving through wild countryside and primitive villages from Merida to the coast, and finally along a rutty dirt driveway, the most striking sight is a crumbling cement tower that, in handpainted letters, proclaims this spot to be the CLUB DE PATOS. This moment of skeptical wonder is reinforced by your first glance at the cement block club house. It looks deserted.

But all is well. In fact, it is very well. Though the grounds and buildings are a bit disheveled, the comfort and beauty of this hunt-

The gardener has a full-time job just watering the flowers and grass around the cabañas.

On the previous page, hunter Don Beck waits expectantly as the first rays of dawn herald the start of another day's hunting. Below, the main building of the club is shown against the brilliant blue of the Yucatan sky.

154

club-by-the-sea far outweigh first impressions. And the hunting at Club de Patos at the northern tip of the Yucatan peninsula is hard to beat.

The location of the club is spectacular. Long, low bungalows stretch out along snowy white sand dunes. Each room has a private porch that faces the broad, shell-strewn beach and the endless Gulf of Mexico. A short walk along the water takes you to the tiny fishing village of Sisal where colorfully painted boats bake in the sun like a legion of rainbow-colored whales. Natives scurry to meet small fishing boats as they unload their burden of glistening red snapper, squid, and yellowtail.

Each morning at three A.M. a gentle knock at the door announces wake up. Immediately after breakfast, vans are loaded with hunters and equipment. Off you go through the wild low brush that

Hunter John Maher, from Los Angeles, at the ready, while his guide summons the ducks with a call. Below he is shown happily displaying his limit.

The locals spend a lot of time at the beach fishing, and club guests go to watch.

The nearby town of Sisal, with a sign "Ice for Sale."

separates beach from miles and miles of shallow inland lagoon. The van finally pulls to a stop and you meet your barefoot native guide who has been waiting in his flat-bottomed boat by the edge of the lagoon. The transfer to the boat is quickly negotiated and the guide begins to pole silently past islands of low-hanging mangrove, which is thickly clustered along the periphery of the still shallows. Out in the open, the reflections of solitary mangrove islands look like clouds floating in the luminous water, blushed pink from the first rays of dawn.

After securing the boat in a mangrove blind, the guide begins his expert calls. Teal, pintail, and sometimes widgeon and muscovy wing through the air and come swiftly to the scattered decoys. The shooting is superb, the guides good-humored and professional, and you discover you've reached your limit long before mid-morning.

*The happy hunters of
Club de Patos gathered
at the pool for
this portrait.*

Back at the club you have the choice of a swim in the butterfly-shaped swimming pool, an invigorating dip in the Gulf, or a well-deserved nap before lunch. After lunch, those shooters interested in quail set out for the afternoon. Hunting quail in the Yucatan is rigorous. Proper protective clothing, sturdy boots, and *stamina* are prerequisites for a successful day but the effort is handsomely rewarded because wild quail are plentiful. A great bonus for sports fishermen is a tarpon pond that is hidden in the shallows of the backwater. A word to the manager and the trip is arranged.

Food at the club is delicious. Dinner usually begins with a first course of soup or pasta and moves on to perfectly cooked smoked pork chops, breast of chicken marinated in a tangy sauce, braised duck, grilled fish, or roast quail. Pan Français, the Mexican equivalent to French bread, and limitless, excellent cold beer are staples.

Accommodations at Club de Patos are spare, clean, and comfortable. Each room contains two double beds with firm mattresses, loads of closet and drawer space, and a bathroom. Once you slip between fresh, clean sheets, the sound of the waves crashing onto the beach lulls you to sleep—to dream of another day of hunting at this idyllic site.

*One of the locals,
who acts as a retriever.*

VERMEJO

PARK RANCH

Raton,
New Mexico

One of the world's great sports and nature lodges.

VERMEJO PARK RANCH is magnificent beyond words. Every cliché-ridden adjective in Webster's dictionary could aptly apply to the beauty of the scenery, the sheer abundance of nature, and yet not capture the ineffable essence of wonder encompassed in these 392,000 acres of northern New Mexican wilderness. The Sangre de Cristo mountains, purple and tan and iced with snow, predominate, but are tempered and softened by alpine meadows of tawny grass. Ponderosa and piñon pine, juniper and Douglas fir fill the crystal air with their fresh fragrance. In autumn, brushy Gamble's oak and elegant aspen paint broad swatches of brilliant orange and gold across the face of each towering reach. Elk, mule deer, black bear, bison, mountain lion, and antelope reside here, as do wild turkey, scaled quail, green-winged, blue-winged, and cinnamon teal, mallard, mourning dove, and the Canada goose. As an added starter, rainbow, cutthroat, and brook trout are available in the various lakes and streams. Visitors to Vermejo indulge in a taste of the crème de la crème of hunting and fishing resorts.

The lodge at Vermejo came into being early in the century after Chicago grain speculator William H. Bartlett purchased the tract

The ranch is a game-watcher's paradise. On the previous page is a four-year-old elk that will grow into next year's trophy. Here are two members of a thriving herd of great plains bison, or buffalo, as they are commonly called.

Mule deer, which are staging a dramatic comeback at Vermejo.

Texan Clayton Williams with his trophy elk, a magnificent 6 × 6 specimen that has six points on each antler.

from the Maxwell Land Grant Company. With partner H.W. Adams, Bartlett established a cattle ranch, brought elk to Vermejo to reestablish the dwindling herds, and built a fish hatchery to support a series of beautiful lakes. Meanwhile Bartlett created three tile-roofed stone mansions to house himself and his many guests in grand style. In 1926 Vermejo Park became an elite private retreat known as the Vermejo Club, numbering Douglas Fairbanks, Herbert Hoover, Calvin Coolidge, Andrew Mellon, F.W. Kellogg, Cecil B. DeMille, and Harvey Firestone, among others, as members. During the Depression, the Club disbanded and Vermejo was bought by Fort Worth businessman W.J. Gourley.

Today, Vermejo Park is, without doubt, one of the finest sports and nature lodges in the world. Quality begins with management.

The ranch abounds in stunning scenery. This view of Ash Mountain illustrates the Spanish word "Vermejo," or "vermillion colored," from which the name derives.

165

The corral at Cimarron, where the ranch's cattle are driven after being rounded up for sale. In the corral with them are Pennzoil vice president Paul Rundle and lawyer Donald Duncan.

Owned by the Houston-based Pennzoil Company, all energies are focused on the pursuit of intelligent land- and game-management practices. As in the days of Bartlett and Adams, Vermejo remains a working cattle ranch. Though the cowboys ride, rope, and brand, many also hold college degrees in animal husbandry or land management. Vermejo's wildlife biologist, Gary Wolfe, monitors and improves the habitat of the park's wildlife population. Lucky sportsmen reap the benefits of this constant vigilance.

The premier sport at Vermejo is hunting trophy bull elk, and the atmosphere surrounding the first hunt of the year, early in October, is electric. With only 26 hunters taking part, this hunt must be booked two years in advance. Five additional elk hunts, which run from mid-October to the first of December, are offered as well, and the success rate for each is astoundingly high. Vermejo manager Louis Kestenbaum laughs wryly when he says that this success rate is their biggest problem. "With our odds, hunters come here *expecting* to get their trophy. Those few who miss an elk tend to get their egos bent out of shape." Now this is the kind of problem most lodges dream of!

Besides offering what is probably the finest elk hunt in existence, the ranch organizes guided hunts for mule deer, antelope, black

One of the sitting rooms at Casa Grande, the original home that William Bartlett built for himself.

Headquarters Lodge, much-used throughout the year.

166

bear, mountain lion, and turkey. The challenge is very real. Vermejo uses no game-proof fencing—all wildlife is strictly free-roaming.

As might be expected, visitors "rough it" in style. Guests might stay at Bartlett's original getaway, known simply as Headquarters. Two of his three mansions still stand, with several solid and comfortable guest cottages completing the compound. Besides the plush Headquarters, two separate rustic camps—Costilla and Cresmer—accommodate groups of hunters and fishermen. Costilla, at about 10,000 feet, commands a sweeping view of the Costilla vega, stream, and the mountains. Cresmer, which nestles in the pines at some 8800 feet, is situated at the edge of the lake country and is a favorite of fishermen.

The interior of Cresmer Lodge, very rustic and in use during part of the year.

Louis Kestenbaum, manager and host.

Lodge Information

GOLDEN HORN LODGE

GOLDEN HORN LODGE. P.O. Box 6748, Anchorage, AK 99502; (907) 243-1455; Bud and Holly Hodson, part-owners and managers. A fishing lodge in the Alaskan wilderness, open June 1 to October 1. Catch and release, single-hook-only fishing for rainbow trout, grayling, and Arctic char. Outfitting, licensing and guide services. Special clothing should include rain gear and hip boots or waders for fishing.

The lodge contains 10 guest rooms all in one structure, the second largest log building in Alaska. Each room has private shower and bath with good water pressure, a luxury in Alaska. Rates, including 3 meals a day:

$2,500 per person per week, with additional $125 flight fee to and from Dillingham. The dining room has a special charm and there is a bar. Guests may also bring their own liquor. Children welcome. Pets not permitted. Reservations required with a 50% deposit and the balance 30 days before arrival in Dillingham. Personal checks accepted; no credit cards. Recreational facilities consist simply in being there.

DIRECTIONS: Commercial, chartered, or your own wheeled plane from Anchorage to Dillingham. Lodge picks you up in its float plane for trip to lodge, depending on weather.

BRISTOL BAY LODGE

BRISTOL BAY LODGE. P.O. Box 6349, Anchorage, AK 99502; (907) 248-1714; Maggie Garry, owner and Ron McMillan, manager. A fishing lodge in the Alaskan wilderness open June 1 to October 2. Catch and release, single-hook fishing with strict enforcement of state regulation of limits: rainbow trout, Arctic grayling, Arctic char, lake trout, northern pike, Dolly Varden. In addition, there is regular fishing for salmon: chinook in mid-June; chum in late June; sockeye in mid-July; pink in late July; coho in mid-August. There is no licensing available at the lodge, but complete information will be given upon request when reserving. Regarding special clothing, come prepared for anything and everything, including rain, wind, sun, mosquitoes, and cold.

The lodge accommodates 16 people in 2 cabins and

4 guest rooms in the lodge itself, all with modern private baths. There is also a wilderness camp maintained in superb order. Rates, including 2 meals a day, with bag lunch and snacks: $2,500 per person per week, with $1,000 deposit and balance 60 days before arrival. There is a bar, and guests may also bring their own liquor. Children welcome, but there is no special rate. Pets not welcome. Personal checks accepted, but no credit cards. Recreational facilities are limited to volleyball and horseshoes; fishing is the name of the game here.

DIRECTIONS: There is daily 737 jet service between Anchorage and Dillingham. The lodge will meet you with its float plane on arrival at Dillingham, depending on weather.

PLUMMER'S LODGES

PLUMMER'S LODGES. 1110 Sanford Street, Winnipeg, Manitoba, Canada R3E 2Z9; (204) 772-8833; C. "Chummy" Plummer, owner and manager. The main lodge supplies fishing for lake trout and Arctic grayling on Great Bear Lake, 47 miles north of the Arctic Circle in Canada's Northwest Territories. The outcamp at Coronation bay on the Arctic ocean offers the best fishing in the world for Arctic char. Outfitting, licensing, and guide services available at Great Bear Lake. It is fairly cold, even in the summer, so warm clothing is a must.

There are 21 guest accommodations with private, semi-modern baths. Rates, including excellent meals: $1975 (U.S.) per person per week, including air transportation from Winnipeg, Manitoba. Flying oneself to the lodge, $175 per day per person. Extra for Coronation Bay outcamp. Liquor is served, but guests may bring their own. Children welcome (no special rates). Pets not permitted. Personal checks accepted. No credit cards.

DIRECTIONS: Boeing 737 flight leaves Winnipeg every Saturday, and takes 3½ hours to Great Bear Lake.

FRONTIER FISHING LODGE

FRONTIER FISHING LODGE. P.O. Box 4550, Edmonton, Alberta, Canada T6E 5G4; (403) 433-4914 in winter, (403) 370-3501 in summer; Jerry Bricker, owner and manager. A remote fishing lodge on the Great Slave Lake in Canada's Northwest Territories, open mid-June through mid-September. The use of barbless and single hooks is suggested for lake trout, Arctic grayling, northern pike, and whitefish. The lodge has a tackle shop, a store for clothing, and provides local Chipewyan Indians as guides.

A variety of log cabins sleep 24 to 42 guests, with private and shared baths. Rates, including meals: $1,640 (U.S.) per person per week, Saturday to Saturday, including transportation from Yellowknife; $230 (U.S.) per person per day for those who fly themselves to lodge (enquire about landing strip details). There is a dining room with a French-Canadian chef for lodge guests only. Liquor is served, but it is sold by the bottle or guests may bring their own. Children welcome (no special rates). Pets not permitted. Personal checks accepted. No credit cards.

DIRECTIONS: Commercial aircraft from Edmonton to Yellowknife. Lodge provides air transportation from there to the lodge.

CORBETT LAKE COUNTRY INN

CORBETT LAKE COUNTRY INN. P.O. Box 327, Merritt, British Columbia, Canada V0K 2B0; (604) 378-4334; Peter McVey, owner and manager. A fishing lodge in the Thompson-Nicola region of the interior of the province, open May 1 to October 4 and Christmas Eve to March 1. Fly fishing for rainbow trout (also known as Kamloops trout in this area) from unpowered boats. Licenses available in Merritt. Climate in summer hot during the day, evenings cool down to 40 degrees F.

There are 7 cabins of log construction, with heaters and fireplaces and private baths. Additional 3 guest rooms are available in the basement of the central lodge building. Rates: $40 per person in cabins; $34 per person in rooms. Fine dining on gourmet cooking for guests and public, with extensive wine list. Lounge bar serves liquor. Guests may also bring their own. Children welcome, with reduced prices for special children's meals. Pets welcome. Checks accepted, but no credit cards. Recreation facilities include skeet shooting and hiking. Riding horses can be made available.

DIRECTIONS: 12 miles south of Merritt on Rte. 5. Watch for sign on highway.

STEAMBOAT INN

STEAMBOAT INN. Toketee Route Box 36, Idleyld Park, OR 97447; (503) 496-3495; Jim and Sharon Van Loan, owners and managers. A hospitable fishing lodge open year around, specializing in fly fishing for steelhead trout, with outfitting, licensing, and guide services available at lodge. Rain gear and warm clothing are suggested for the damp and rainy climate.

There are 8 guest rooms with 2 double beds each and private baths. Rates: $48 per day, double only; additional adults $12. Rooms payable in advance when making reservation. Meals extra, served 7 days. Dining open to public. Wine and beer available, but guests may bring their own. Children welcome. Pets discouraged. Visa and MasterCard accepted. Money credited to account on cancellations two weeks or more in advance of reservation date.

DIRECTIONS: From Eugene, Oregon, take I-5 south to Rte. 138. Go east on 138 to the inn, which is 24 miles of scenic driving after the highway narrows to 2 lanes, and signs of civilization have disappeared.

HOT CREEK RANCH

HOT CREEK RANCH. Route 1, Box 206, Mammoth Lakes, CA 93546; (619) 935-4214; owned by the Ray Bateman family; Lee and Rosetta Willardson, managers. An exquisitely situated fishing lodge open from the last Saturday in April until the 31st of October, specializing in brown trout and rainbow trout under a catch-and-release program using barbless hooks and dry flies only. Outfitting, licensing, and guide service available, except for rods, which guests must bring. Guests should be warned that the sun's rays at 7,100 feet elevation are much hotter than at lower altitudes.

There are 9 housekeeping cottages with 2 double beds each, all with modern baths. Rates (subject to annual change): *Weekdays,* Sunday through Wednesday, $54 per day for two people, 2-day minimum; $20 per day for each additional guest. *Weekend,* minimum 3 days, $187 for 2 people; $59 for each additional guest. *Weekly,* $340 for 2 people. Deposit required on all reservations; 2 weeks notice required on cancellations. Before April 15, call Lee Willardson at (619) 582-6028 or write 5631 Dorothy Way, San Diego, CA 92115 for reservations. Children welcome (under 10 years $5 per day; 10 through 15 years, $9 per day). There is no food served at the ranch, and there is no bar. Guests may bring their own liquor and food, and there are adequate dining facilities in town. Personal checks accepted. No credit cards. Recreation includes horseback riding and trapshooting. Nearby there is swimming in the public hot springs.

DIRECTIONS: From Bishop, California, north on U.S. 395 to Mammoth Lakes. Turn right toward airport and continue past airport entrance about 1 mile until the "Hot Creek" sign appears.

MIDDLE FORK LODGE

MIDDLE FORK LODGE. Box 10, Reno, NV 89504; (702) 786-3232. Lewis A. (Bud) Kellow, manager. A hunting and fishing lodge in Idaho's River of No Return Wilderness, accessible only by airplane. Open from April to November for hunting mule deer, mountain lion, bear, bighorn sheep, mountain goat, elk, and fishing for cutthroat, rainbow, and Dolly Varden trout under catch-and-release program. Out-of-state hunters must apply for license before August first of the preceding season.

A luxurious lodge with 6 cabins, 1 river house, and guest rooms in the lodge itself, all with modern, private baths. Rates, including 3 sumptuous meals: Sunday through Thursday, $125 per adult per night; Friday and Saturday, $150 per adult per night; group rates of 8 or more, $99 per adult on weekdays, $125 per adult on weekends. Two-night minimum including flight in and out of Boise. Rates at the door: $99 per adult. Beer and wine only are served. Children welcome; no charge for children under 6; children 6–15 half-price. Pets not accepted. Recreation facilities include horseback riding, river rafting, skeet shooting, ping pong, pool, swimming in heated pool.

DIRECTIONS: Lodge picks up in own airplane at Boise airport: Harrah's Middle Fork Charters, 4888 Aeronca Street, Boise, ID 83705. Telephone (208) 342-7888.

CRESCENT H RANCH

CRESCENT H RANCH. Rivermeadows Inc., P.O. Box 347, Wilson, WY 83014; (307) 733-3674 or 733-2841. Don Albrecht, owner; Vern Bressler, resident manager. A hunting and fishing lodge open from June 1 to October 15. Fall hunting for elk, mule deer, moose, bighorn sheep. Fly fishing only for cutthroat, rainbow, and brown trout. Complete outfitting, licensing, guide services available; tackle shop on premises. Special packages include: 5-day *Fly Fishing School;* 5 days of *Fly Fishing;* 2 weeks of *Fly Fishing;* for young people— *Outdoorsman Fly Fishing Program* (boys 14 to 18); *Outdoorsman Explorer Program* (boys 14 to 18 graduated from Outdoorsman Fly Fishing Program); *Rivermeadows Adventure Program* (girls 12 to 14).

Rivermeadows Inc. consists of two ranches, Crescent H in Wyoming and Firehole in Montana. The review here concerns the most popular, Crescent H, which has 10 log cabins with modern baths. Rates, including breakfast, sack lunches and gourmet dining: single $150 per day; double $110 per person; triple $95 per person; children under 12, $90. Guests may invite dinner guests with permission. There is an open bar; guests may also bring their own liquor. Children are welcome. Pets are not normally accepted. Cash or personal checks only accepted. Recreation facilities include horseback riding, hiking, skeet shooting, wildlife photography.

DIRECTIONS: In western Wyoming 10 miles from Jackson. Take Rte. 22 from Jackson to Wilson and Fall Creek from Wilson to Crescent H Ranch.

MABEL'S ISLAND

MABEL'S ISLAND. c/o Douglas Kenyon, 155 East Ohio Street, Chicago, IL 60611; (312) 642-5300; Douglas Kenyon, owner. A fishing and hunting lodge in the Lake-of-the-Woods region of Ontario, Canada, open June 1 to October 30. Duck hunting, deer hunting, and fishing for lake trout, walleye, northern pike, muskie, or smallmouth bass. Complete outfitting, including guns, rods, included in rates. License available locally. Limited at any one time to one party of five or less.

A classic hunting lodge accommodating five guests maximum. Rates: $250 per person per day, with a three-day minimum, including all meals and equipment. Liquor provided or guests may bring own. Children welcome (no reduced rate). Pets welcome. No credit cards accepted. Deposit in advance with reservation; balance as arranged. Recreation includes swimming, water skiing, snorkeling, horseshoes.

DIRECTIONS: Chartered float plane from International Falls, Minnesota, as arranged with owner.

FORTEAU SALMON LODGE

FORTEAU SALMON LODGE. L'Anse au Clair, Labrador, Newfoundland AOK 3KO, Canada; (709) 931-2332 or 2862; Steve and Shirley Letto, owner-managers. A fishing lodge located in a relatively accessible part of southern Labrador on the Forteau River, which teems with Atlantic salmon from July to September. Open June 15 to September 15 primarily for salmon fishing, but speckled trout and sea trout are obtainable. Limit is 2 salmon per day. Both wet and dry flies will be used, eights and ten in July and tens and twelves in August, with single or double hooks. Best patterns in wets are Black Silvertips, tied with moose or bear hair, and White and Grey Wulff in dries. Bring also 6 to 10 lb. test leaders, a good floating fly line, rod and reel, warm clothing, raincoat, waders, and mosquito repellent. Flies are also available at the lodge. License and guide supplied at lodge. Visa, MasterCard, American Express cards accepted.

There are 6 double rooms with shared baths in the lodge, as well as a lounge and dining room. Rates, including homestyle meals: $1050 per week or $150 per day for shorter stays. License $40 extra. Liquor available if ordered before arrival. Not all brands obtainable and very expensive. Children of all ages welcome, but no pets. For entertainment, there are 4 nightclubs in nearby towns and cod jigging in the Strait of Belle Isle.

DIRECTIONS: Blanc Sablon in Quebec is the closest center, 12 miles from the lodge. Labrador Airways flies from Gander-St. John's and Deer Lake, Newfoundland and Goose Bay, Labrador, and Quebec Air flies from Montreal. There is also a car ferry to Blanc Sablon from St. Barbe, Newfoundland, which is a 300-mile drive from Port aux Basques, where the ferry from North Sydney, Nova Scotia brings you. North Sydney is on Cape Breton, the easternmost part of Nova Scotia.

WADE'S FISHING LODGE

WADE'S FISHING LODGE. Blackville, New Brunswick, Canada; (506) 843-2288, Blackville exchange; October 1 to April 1, 143 Main Street, Fredericton, N.B. E3A 1C6; (506) 472-6454; Herb Wade, owner-manager. A salmon-fishing lodge situated on the famous Miramichi River. Open April 15 to September 30 for spring and summer runs of Atlantic salmon. Limit of 2 per day, including released fish. There is one guide per guest. Lodge provides everything from equipment to waders to licenses, but suggests bringing rain gear, hats, and bug repellent.

Parties are housed in individual cabins with separate bedrooms and private baths, for a total of 20 people at any one time. Rates, including all meals and guide services: $170 (Can.) per day per person. Deposits of $100 per person required at least 30 days prior to arrival, or with confirmation if less than 30 days. Parties of 2 or more preferred. Children welcome, but nothing to do except fishing. No pets. No credit cards, but checks accepted.

DIRECTIONS: Commercial flights to Fredericton, N.B. and 90-minute drive to lodge. Private aircraft fly to Upper Blackville Airport and 15-mile drive. To drive, take Rte. 8 north from Fredericton to Blackville. At Blackville, turn right at Post Office and follow signs.

LEEN'S LODGE

LEEN'S LODGE. Grand Lake Stream, ME 04412; (207) 796-5575; winter address between October and May, Box 100, Brewer, ME 04412; (207) 989-7363; Stanley Leen, owner-manager. A fishing lodge in the Grand Lake region of eastern Maine, open May 1 to late September. Fishing for landlocked salmon, small mouth bass, togue or lake trout, brook trout, white perch, and pickerel. Fishing licenses obtainable at the lodge, along with equipment rentals and a small amount of gear.

The lodge consists of 10 cabins of various sizes sleeping 2 to 8 people. All cabins have a living room with fireplace, separate bedrooms, full baths, and automatic heat.

Rates, including full breakfast and dinner: $48 per person per day. Family plan on request. Lunch provided at a small additional cost, plus gear for cookouts. Guide service is extra at $75 per day. Lodge dining room caters to special diets, and will cook your catch. Bring your own liquor; main lodge has individually locked liquor cabinets with set-ups available. Children encouraged. Pets accepted. Visa credit card and checks accepted.

DIRECTIONS: From Bangor, Maine, take Rte. 9 east to Baring, then Rte. 1 north to Grand Lake Stream via Woodland and Princeton. Lodge is 1 mile from town.

GARNET HILL LODGE

GARNET HILL LODGE. North River, NY 12856; (518) 251-2821; George and Mary Heim, owner-managers. A hunting and fishing lodge open all year except for 10 days at Thanksgiving and 10 days in June. Game hunted is whitetail deer, black bear, and grouse; major fish are landlocked salmon (1 per day) and brook trout (3 per day). Deer season with rifles usually begins second-last Saturday in October with limit of 1 per hunter; black powder opens 1 week before rifle season, and bow opens before black powder. Bear season runs from September into first week of December. Fishing season runs from ice-out sometime in April until September 30. Recommend bringing own equipment, except for boats and canoes. Guides, highly recommended for all sports, can be provided through lodge upon advance notification. Licenses available from town clerk Monday through Saturday. Black fly season in May-June requires plenty of repellent.

The main lodge is a log house with 14 rooms, accommodating 2 to 3 people each, with private and shared baths. Rooms are not sound-proof: bring ear plugs if you are a light sleeper. Another lodge, Big Shanty, has 7 rooms sleeping 20, 1 with private bath and the others sharing 3 baths. Rates, including breakfast and dinner: $32-36 per day, double occupancy: $10 extra for single; $22 extra for additional person in room. Full luncheon is served and full bar service is available. Children welcome; those under 10 sharing room with parents, $17 per day. No pets. Personal checks accepted, but no credit cards.

DIRECTIONS: From New York City north on I-87 past Albany, Saratoga, and Lake George to Warrensburg, exit 23. At Warrensburg north on Rte. 9 for 4.5 miles, then northwest on Rte. 28 to Wevertown. From Wevertown continue on Rte. 28 for 11.5 miles past North River general store and post office to 13th Lake Rd. Turn left for 4.1 miles to Garnet Hill Rd., which branches left. Take Garnet Hill Rd. for .4 miles and turn left to lodge for .2 miles.

BURNT PINE PLANTATION

BURNT PINE PLANTATION. 2121 Newmarket Parkway, Suite 134, Marietta, GA 30067; (404) 953-0326; lodge (404) 342-2170; David Morse, owner; Lawrence Wood, general manager. A quail and deer preserve carefully managed for ideal hunting. Open for quail October 1 through March 31; deer from mid-October to first part of December and December 26 to January 1. Deer bow season mid-September to mid-October; can hunt with bows during gun season, but under gun laws. Lodge sells needed licenses and shotgun shells and provides guide services. Write for list of recommended clothing and equipment.

Burnt Pine has a main hunting lodge with 3 bedrooms sleeping 8 and 2 small lodges each sleeping 6, with private baths. Rates, per day: lodging and 3 meals, $55; DEER HUNTS (limit of 2), archery $115; firearms $175 (buck), $195 (either sex); QUAIL HUNTS, $175 (with guides, field transportation, and dogs), $100 (without),

$75 (half-day without); COMBINATION HUNTS, $245. Other services provided, such as dressing, cleaning, trap shooting, gun rental, etc. Reservations require deposit of $100 per day per hunter, refundable if cancelled not less than 30 days before hunt. Dry county—bring your own liquor, but drinking only after hunting at end of day. Children under 14 discouraged and under 16 for deer hunting discouraged. An authorized guardian must be withing touching distance at all times. For those who bring their own dogs there is a special preserve with no guides. Must have health certificate for dogs to be boarded, but boarding is discouraged.

DIRECTIONS: I-20 east from Atlanta to Madison-Monticello exit; drive south on Rte. 83 for 7 miles to Little River bridge; cross and continue 2 more miles, then turn right on paved road with planted pines on both sides; drive 1.5 miles to "Burnt Pine" sign and lodge on right.

TELICO JUNCTION HUNTING PRESERVE

TELICO JUNCTION HUNTING PRESERVE. Hog Hollow Road, Englewood, TE 37329; (615) 887-7819; Joe and Mazie Meeks, owner-managers. A fenced hunting preserve in the heart of the Great Smoky Mountains wilderness. The specialty is wild boar—Russian and razorback—which make excellent trophies prepared by the taxidermy service on the preserve. There are also fallow and sika deer, Mauna Kea or white ram, native to Hawaii, Barbedow ram native to Corsica, Catalina and Spanish goats, and wild Tom turkey. Kills are guaranteed with use of standard deer hunting rifle for animals and 20 gauge or larger shotguns using number 2, 4, or 6 shot for turkeys. Guides provided as part of fee.

Accommodations for up to 17 persons are in two furnished trailers and two apartments with cooking facili-

ties, as no food is served. Rates: 2-day hunts for all animals are $300 except goat, which are $250 each, and trophy Tom turkey, $100, or non-trophy Tom or hen, $75, as extras to regular hunts. There is a charge of $50 per day expenses for hunters who fail to achieve their guaranteed kill. This applies very rarely. Licenses are included in hunt costs. Hunters may arrive Sundays or Wednesdays after 4 P.M. Non-hunting wives free. Other non-hunters $10 per night depending on space. No alcohol of any kind permitted on property. Non-returnable $50 deposit required with reservation. No personal checks or credit cards accepted.

DIRECTIONS: 4.5 miles from Englewood, which is south of Knoxville on U.S. 411. Private planes can use McMinn County airport 7 miles away.

PORT OF THE ISLANDS

PORT OF THE ISLANDS. Rte. 41, Marco, FL 33937; out-of-state (800) 237-4173 or (813) 394-3101; David Botbol, manager. A fishing and hunting lodge-resort open all year with fishing for snook, redfish, tarpon, snapper, flounder, sea trout, black grouper; hunting for wild hog, deer, turkey; ranges for skeet and trap, pistol and rifle, running boar. Fishing licenses, gun and ammo rental, and fishing gear rental all available.

There are 184 rooms in the complex, all with private showers and baths. Rates: high season $60 to $115, sin-

gle or double; off-season $45 to $100 single or double. Children under 15 free. Modified American plan $25 per person. Boat rentals $45 per day; fishing guides $150 per day for two people. No pets. Visa, MasterCard, American Express cards accepted.

DIRECTIONS: There is a private landing strip at the lodge, which, otherwise, is a 90-minute drive from Miami across the peninsula on U.S. 41 to Royal Palm Hammock and Rte. 92 southwest to Marco.

CHEECA LODGE

CHEECA LODGE. P.O. Box 527, U.S. 1, Mile Marker 82, Islamorada, FL 33036; (305) 664-4651, Miami direct line 245-3755, from out-of-state (800) 327-2888; Harry Galloway, manager. A luxurious fishing lodge and resort in the Florida Keys specializing in bonefish, permit, and deepsea tarpon and sailfish for sport and grouper, snapper, and sea trout for eating. Outfitting and guide service available. No license necessary for saltwater fishing. Guides must be arranged for well in advance.

There are 86 units, all with private baths (some showers only). Rates: high season December to April, $145 to $175; off-season, $100 to $120. Full restaurant and bar. Special activities for children. Accept all major credit cards. Lodge arranges fishing expeditions separately with Islamorada marinas. Typical range for boat charters, including tackle, bait, and crew, per day: deep sea, $375 to $425 up to 6 people; back country, $185 to $200 for 2 people.

DIRECTIONS: On Atlantic Ocean side of Overseas Highway at mile marker 82, on an island 1.5 hour drive south of Miami.

CLUB DE PATOS

CLUB DE PATOS. Sisal, Yucatan, Mexico; c/o Larry Adams, 4610 Amberly Court North, Atlanta, GA 30360; (404) 451-2426; Victor Valez, owner; Larry Adams, American representative. A hunting lodge on the Gulf of Mexico open all year. Specializing in duck hunting for blue-wing teal, green-wing teal, some cinnamon teal, blue bill, ring neck, pin tail, widgeon, and now and again, a Muscovy. Quail are also available, and there is a tarpon hole for sports fishermen. Limit on duck is 15, which may be brought into U.S. No limit on quail, which must be eaten at club as they cannot be imported. Outfitting and licensing provided at club, but bring light camouflage clothing, sturdy boots, mosquito repellent, and hat. Remington 1100 guns are provided; bringing guns into Mexico is very difficult, but can be done as follows: give Larry Adams at least 45 days notice, along with model number, make, serial number, gauge, passport photo, and a letter from your local sheriff or mayor. Club provides guide service.

Lodge provides 12 double rooms with private baths. Rates, including meals and unlimited beer: $675 for 3-day hunt, plus $30 license, $30 conservation stamp, $10 per day gun rental. Quail hunting is $40 extra per day. Non-hunters $425 for 3 days. All shells and liquor provided at extra charge. Animals require 45 days notice for paperwork, and proof of shots from your vet. School-age children accepted at full rates except at Christmas, when there is a special rate for fathers and sons, when children go at the non-hunter rate. Checks accepted, but no credit cards.

DIRECTIONS: Commercial flights to Merida from Houston, Miami, or Mexico City. Club van picks you up there and brings you back.

VERMEJO PARK RANCH

VERMEJO PARK RANCH. P.O. Drawer E, Raton, NM 87740; (505) 445-3097 or 5028; Pennzoil Company, owners; Louis Kestenbaum and Gary Wolfe, managers. A 392,000-acre working ranch committed to wildlife management and conservation. Hereford cattle co-exist with buffalo, elk, deer, cougar, wild turkey, antelope, bear, beaver, small game, various species of birds, and rainbow, cutthroat, and brook trout. Open during elk and deer season from early October to late December, turkey season in early April to May 1, rest of summer until late September for fishing and antelope (early Sept.)

Lodging and meals are provided at a number of lodges with dining rooms and are fully staffed with cooks, waitresses and maids. There are lodges at different elevations for specific types of hunts. Rates per hunt, including lodging, meals, bar tab, trespass permit, hunting license, guides, 4-wheel drive vehicles, skinning and quartering of game, and state sales tax; ELK, $4,500; ANTELOPE, $1,350; MULE DEER, $2,000. Turkey hunts and fishing charged on a daily rate of $100 to $150 per person, including lodging, meals, and permit. Bear and lion rates on application. The ranch provides a great deal of information and advice relating to the various hunts and activities. Deposit required on reservation is 50%. Limited accommodation for non-hunters at $1,000 each. Children accepted. No pets. Checks accepted.

DIRECTIONS: I-25 south from Denver to Raton, New Mexico, in the northeast part of the state. Ranch is 40 miles west of Raton on Rte. 555, which begins south of town near La Mesa race track. Private and chartered planes can fly to Crews Field, 10 miles southwest of Raton. Ranch will pick up there.